D1436458

TORCH BIBLE
COMMENTARIES

General Editors

THE REV. JOHN MARSH, D.PHIL.
Principal of Mansfield College, Oxford

THE REV. DAVID M. PATON, M.A.
Editor, SCM Press

THE REV. ALAN RICHARDSON, D.D.
Professor of Christian Theology in the University of Nottingham

FOREWORD TO SERIES

The aim of this series of commentaries on books of the Bible is to provide the general reader with the soundest possible assistance in understanding the message of each book considered as a whole and as a part of the Bible.

The findings and views of modern critical scholarship on the text of the Bible have been taken fully into account. Indeed, it is our view that only on a basis of sound scholarship can the message of the Bible be fully understood. But minute points of scholarship, of language or archaeology or text, have not been pushed into the foreground. We have asked the writers of the various books to have in mind the view that the Bible is more than a quarry for the practice of erudition; that it contains the living message of the living God.

The 'general' reader whom we wish to help is therefore not only of one type. We hope that intelligent people of varying interests will find that these commentaries, while not ignoring the surface difficulties, are able to concentrate the mind on the essential Gospel contained in the various books of the Bible. In brief, the TORCH BIBLE COMMENTARIES are for the thoughtful reader who wishes to understand his Bible.

Volumes in the series include:

ST PAUL'S EPISTLES TO THE

THESSALONIANS

Introduction and Commentary

by

WILLIAM NEIL
M.A., B.D., Ph.D.

*Warden of Hugh Stewart Hall
and Lecturer in Biblical Studies in the
University of Nottingham*

SCM PRESS LTD

56 BLOOMSBURY STREET LONDON WC1

First published 1957

Printed in Great Britain by
Northumberland Press Limited
Gateshead on Tyne

CONTENTS

COMMENTARY

THE FIRST EPISTLE TO THE THESSALONIANS

I

THANKS BE TO GOD 1.1-10

II

PAUL DEFENDS HIS RECORD 2.1-16

III

FOLLOW-UP TO THE MISSION 2.17-3.13

IV

SOME SPECIAL PROBLEMS 4.1-5.22

V

★

THE SECOND EPISTLE TO THE THESSALONIANS

I

II

III

PREFACE

There would seem to be little excuse for a commentator writing a second commentary on the same book of the Bible within ten years, especially since so far as I know no major changes in the critical approach to the Thessalonian letters have emerged since my Moffatt commentary was published in 1950. My only excuse for the present work can therefore be that its shorter compass has enabled me to concentrate more on the religious significance of these letters, on the assumption that, where critical questions are glossed over, readers who are interested in these matters will refer to the more detailed treatment which I have given them in the Moffatt series.

As we all know to our cost, the danger of a critical commentary which tries to take into account all the previous work that has been done on the subject is that it sometimes prevents us from seeing the wood for the trees. There is obviously room and need for both types of commentary and while it is impossible for the same writer commenting on the same Biblical books not to echo some of his previous ideas and phrases, I have tried to interpret these fascinating letters afresh, having uppermost in my mind all the time that in the admirable words of the General Foreword to the Torch series they contain ' the living message of the living God '.

W.N.

University of Nottingham
January 1957

BIBLIOGRAPHY

The following English Commentaries on the Epistles to the Thessalonians provide a more detailed exposition and study of the text:

G. MILLIGAN, *St. Paul's Epistles to the Thessalonians*
J. E. FRAME *(International Critical Commentaries)*
J. DENNEY *(Expositor's Bible)*
J. MOFFATT *(Expositor's Greek Testament)*
E. J. BICKNELL *(Westminster Commentaries)*
W. NEIL *(Moffatt N.T. Commentaries)*

The following books are useful for further study of the eschatological passages in the epistles:

H. A. A. KENNEDY, *St Paul's Conceptions of the Last Things*
H. H. ROWLEY, *The Relevance of Apocalyptic*
S. B. FROST, *Old Testament Apocalyptic*
T. F. GLASSON, *The Second Advent*
H. A. GUY, *The New Testament Doctrine of the 'Last Things'*

INTRODUCTION

THE THESSALONIAN LETTERS

If we accept the view which is generally held that the Pastoral Epistles are only in a minor degree the actual words of St Paul, we should probably agree that the Thessalonian letters are the least significant of the apostle's writings. They do not play upon the great themes of Romans, Galatians or Ephesians, nor do they give us the fascinating insights into the life of the early Church and the mind of St Paul which the Corinthian letters provide. Although they were probably among the first letters that the apostle wrote they have found their place in the New Testament at the end of the Pauline section, and it would seem to be a not unfitting place.

FIRST IMPRESSIONS

At first sight they appear to deal so exclusively with a particular situation at a particular stage in the Church's history that their message and relevance are not immediately obvious. The apostle is not grappling with problems of high theology, or attempting to interpret the Jewish idiom of the earliest form of the gospel in more universal terms. Such theology as there is is tacitly assumed, except on the matter of the doctrine of the Last Things, and there the form in which it is expressed is so bewildering and obscure that most of us prefer to by-pass it altogether.

13

For the rest, the practical problems of Jewish opposition
to the Christian mission, or Second Adventist hysteria,
which play a prominent part in these letters, do not immediately awaken a response in our minds as being directly
relevant to our own situation.

A TRUER ASSESSMENT

But this is a hasty judgment, as closer attention to the
contents of the Thessalonian letters will prove. They afford
us a most valuable glimpse of a small Christian community finding its feet and facing its problems in a hostile or
indifferent world. They give us a new insight into the mind
and methods of Paul himself, revealing his concern for
every aspect of the life of the people he had brought face
to face with the love of God in Christ; his tact, his sympathy, his shrewdness. Above all they remind us that however deep we have to dig beneath the unfamiliar language
in which it is expressed in order to reach its essential nature,
the element of hope in a purpose of God that reaches
beyond the frontiers of our normal experience has been
embedded firmly in the heart of the Christian gospel from
the beginning.

THESSALONICA

Even in Paul's day Thessalonica, the modern Saloniki,
was a large and prosperous seaport. Lying at the top of
the gulf which bears its name, it looks across an immense
plain to the heights of Mt Olympus, As the capital of
Macedonia in Roman times it had already had a long history. Its older name of Therme, derived from the hot
springs in the neighbourhood, had been changed to Thessalonica in honour of the step-sister of Alexander the Great.
Lying on the great Via Egnatia, the imperial highway

which carried traffic from the East towards Rome, it was a highly cosmopolitan commercial centre. As a free city of the Empire its government was largely autonomous and was administered by politarchs, as the Greek word used in Acts 17.6, 8 indicates, and as inscriptions since discovered there confirm.

PAUL'S SECOND JOURNEY

It was to this important centre that Paul came on his second missionary tour in A.D. 49. He had set out from his headquarters in Antioch in Syria (Acts 15.36 ff.) and had made his way through Asia Minor, visiting en route the churches he had previously founded. For some reason his purpose to evangelize the provinces of Asia and Bithynia was thwarted, and he found himself in the little coastal town of Troas, on the shores of the Aegean, not far from the site of ancient Troy. While there he became convinced that he had been providentially guided to this apparent dead-end, and that he was being called to embark on a more hazardous enterprise in what was to him the unknown territory of Macedonia.

MISSION TO MACEDONIA

His ship landed him at Neapolis, from where he made his way to Philippi and established contact with the small Jewish community. Out of this visit emerged what was probably the first Christian church in Europe. But the mission to Philippi, like so many others in Paul's experience, ended in violent opposition and compulsory withdrawal. The next town to become the centre of a missionary campaign was Thessalonica. It lay seventy miles farther along the Via Egnatia, and had a large enough Jewish community to form a synagogue.

BEGINNING WITH THE SYNAGOGUE

Paul's practice was to direct his attention to the synagogue in the first instance for two reasons. He believed that the Jews, despite their failure to recognize Jesus as the Messiah, were still vital to God's plan of salvation. They must be given a final chance by having the gospel preached to them. Paul's second reason for making contact with the synagogues was a practical one. They generally attracted a fringe congregation of pagan adherents, who, though unprepared to go all the way into Judaism, which involved circumcision and other peculiarly Jewish obligations, were nevertheless attracted by the religion of the Old Testament and found in its wholesome austerity a welcome change from the amoral and superstitious faiths which flourished in the multiplicity of temples and shrines in any city. Such people, familiar with the Law and the Prophets, as with Hebrew Wisdom and Hebrew Psalms, were among the first to respond to a message which offered them all that the Old Testament proclaimed and more, without the cramping limitations which Judaism had imposed upon it.

JEWISH OPPOSITION

It was among such people that Paul found the most ready response. According to the narrative in the Book of Acts (17.1 ff.) his mission to the synagogue of Thessalonica lasted only a few weeks. Some of the Jews were persuaded, but his message was much more effective among the pagan adherents. Before long the Jews who were loyal to the old faith and regarded Paul as a traitor, and who viewed with dismay the defection of their Gentile supporters, stirred up a riot in the city, as a result of which it was thought advisable for Paul to make a hasty and secret departure. The ill-will of these Jews pursued him to his next place of campaign, Beroea, fifty miles further on, and once more he had to make a hurried escape, this time to Athens.

PAGAN RESPONSE

From St Luke's narrative, as well as from the contents of the letters, it appears that he was accompanied at this stage by Silvanus and Timothy. What is not so clear is whether the campaign at Thessalonica lasted only over ' three sabbaths '. It is possible that in the account given in Acts this period refers to the first stage of the campaign, which centred on the synagogue. Two pieces of evidence in the letters would suggest that the mission lasted longer— perhaps a few months. One is the fact that Paul was long enough in Thessalonica to take a regular job, presumably at his own trade, and despite that to need financial assistance from his Philippian friends on more than one occasion (Phil. 4.16). There is the further point that the people to whom Paul writes these letters appear to have been out and out pagans. They had been worshippers of idols (I. 1-9) which would suggest neither Jews nor devout Gentile adherents of the synagogue.

A RICH HARVEST

It is impossible to estimate the success of the mission in terms of numbers. Probably the congregation which resulted from the mission was neither large nor influential. But the fact that there was a Christian congregation at all was for Paul a massive proof of the power of the gospel and a cause for profound thankfulness. There is no reason to doubt that the mission resulted in a marvellous harvest of changed lives or that its results made a profound impression on the whole community (I. 1.7-8). If we are to judge from the summary account in Acts (17.3) the substance of the message which the apostles proclaimed was

the normal gospel testimony of Christian evangelists any-
where. The fact that so much space is devoted in the letters
to questions concerning the end of the world indicates no
more than that this aspect of the apostle's message presented special problems for this particular group of
Christians.

FOLLOW-UP TO THE MISSION

What then was the occasion which necessitated these
letters? The narrative in Acts corresponds with the evidence of the epistles so closely that we can easily follow
the apostle's journey from Thessalonica to Corinth via
Athens. He tells us (I 2.18; 3.2) how he tried more than
once to get back to Thessalonica and how when this
proved impossible he sent Timothy from Athens to build
up the life of the young Thessalonian church. It appears
to have been by no means certain that things would go well
there, owing to strong local opposition. Consequently
when Timothy rejoined Paul at Corinth (Acts 18.5),
bringing welcome news from Thessalonica of the good
progress of the church (I 3.6) and at the same time
reporting certain problems that had arisen, Paul hastened
to write what we now know as the First Epistle to the
Thessalonians.

FIRST LETTER TO THESSALONICA

He begins by giving thanks to God for all that he has
heard from Timothy of the happy sequel to the mission,
and of the growing influence of the Thessalonian Christians
on the life of their country (Ch. 1). But it seems as if an
attempt was being made from outside the little community
to undermine their confidence in the apostle's motives.
Suggestions were apparently being made—probably by the

Jews—that Paul was no better than an itinerant religious charlatan. This he hotly resents and reminds his readers of his behaviour during the mission, in particular of his unwillingness to be dependent on his converts, which entailed carrying on the work of the campaign in what leisure time he could snatch from a hard week's work (Ch. 2). Then he recounts how, since he was unable to visit them himself, he had sent Timothy to strengthen their resistance to the opposition which their conversion to Christianity had aroused, and which had apparently continued ever since the campaign. This he had done although his own position was far from happy (Ch. 3).

PRACTICAL PROBLEMS

Next he turns to some practical problems which it would seem had been reported by Timothy and to which Paul wanted to give immediate attention. First he deals with sex relationships, which were always a problem for Christians drawn from a predominantly pagan society. He states the Christian standard uncompromisingly and leaves it to his readers to apply it to their own circumstances (4.1-8). Then, having touched on the claims of hospitality (4.9-10) and having drawn attention to the desirability of Christians setting a good example of getting on with their jobs quietly and shouldering their fair share of the work of the community (4.11-12), he devotes most of the rest of his letter to two aspects of a doctrinal problem.

DOCTRINAL PROBLEMS

One of the elements of the gospel which was proclaimed in this early stage of the Church's history was the impending end of the world and the return of Christ in Judgment. This would mean the punishment of all the enemies of the truth and the vindication of all who had responded to the

summons to follow Christ. Apparently it was not clear
to the members of the Thessalonian church what would
happen at the Coming of Christ to those of their number
who had died in the meantime. Would they thereby be
deprived of their place among the company of the Lord's
redeemed? Paul gives them the answer (4.13-18) that those
who are still alive at the Lord's Coming will have no
advantage over those who are already dead. Both the living
and the dead who have been faithful to their Lord will
share in his Triumph.

There was a further problem at Thessalonica which was
causing some unsettlement. If the Lord was soon to
return, how could they know when to expect him? Paul's
reply to this (5.1-11) is that this is not given to us to know.
Our Christian duty is simply so to live that we are prepared to face our Maker at any time. Finally, Paul gives
some guidance on the responsibility of the members of the
church towards their leaders, and on the responsibility
of all towards each other, ending with a prayer for God's
blessing on them all and a personal greeting (5.12-28).

SECOND LETTER TO THESSALONICA

It would seem as if this letter did not have the desired
effect and that shortly afterwards Paul had to write again.
This is our Second Epistle to the Thessalonians. It begins
with a reference to the opposition which had apparently
increased at Thessalonica but which was being steadfastly
borne by the members of the little church. Paul reminds
them that to suffer for their faith is an indispensable part
of the Christian life and that there is a divine justice which
redresses the balance either here or hereafter (Ch. 1). He
then returns to the topic dealt with in his previous letter
which still seemed to be upsetting the Thessalonian community, namely the expectation of the Second Advent of

Christ. Considerable excitement had been aroused by the false impression that Paul himself had said that the end of the world was upon them. The apostle hastens to remind them of what he had already told them of the unmistakable signs which would precede the final event of history (2.1-12).

A TENSE SITUATION

Thanking God for the coming into being of the Thessalonian church, and urging them to stand firmly on the teaching they had received (2.13-17), he reminds them of his own difficulties at Corinth and expresses his confidence that they will be guided through their present problems (3.1-5). One of these is the irresponsible behaviour of a few of their own members who in some kind of end-of-the-world hysteria had stopped work and were upsetting the rest of the community. Paul urges that these people should be sharply dealt with, that they should not be supported by the other members of the church, and if need be that they should be cold-shouldered by everybody until they come to their senses (3.6-15). But his last word is an apostolic blessing on the whole congregation (3.16-18).

WHO WROTE THE LETTERS?

The first letter has from the beginning been accepted as a genuinely Pauline epistle. In the heyday of German radical criticism last century its Pauline authorship was disputed, but the consensus of modern scholarship is that the traditional view is correct. The second letter has presented more of a problem. Like the first letter it was accepted by the early Church as an authentic Pauline document, and continued to be accepted as such until last century. Unlike the case of the first letter however the queries which were first raised by the German New Testament scholars at that time are not so easily answered.

PAULINE AUTHORSHIP QUESTIONED

While it is no longer true that scholars find it hard to reconcile the eschatological teaching of the second letter with that of the first, or that it is felt that the figure of Antichrist in II 2.1-12 suggests a later stage in the history of the Church than Paul's day, there are still some difficulties about accepting both letters as being from the hand of the same man.

(a) Some scholars have felt that there is a distinct coolness in the apostle's tone in his second letter which compares oddly with the cordiality of his tone in I Thess.

(b) Others have thought it peculiar that while I Thess. appears to be written to people who have come into the Church directly from paganism, the second letter presupposes an audience which is well versed in the Old Testament and Jewish tradition (cf. II 1.6-10; 2.1-12).

(c) Again, it is remarkable that people so well instructed during the original campaign on matters connected with the Second Coming of Christ should not have known the answer to the problem posed in I 4.13 ff.

(d) It has been further thought to be unlikely that a mind as richly fertile as that of St Paul would be guilty of repeating itself so closely, in places word for word, as is done in these two letters.

MINOR PROBLEMS

It may well be argued that all these objections can be answered.

(a) The coolness of tone is more apparent than real, and such as there is may be the result of pardonable annoyance at a certain amount of unnecessary irresponsibility at Thessalonica.

(b) If the readers of I Thess. had no difficulty in understanding the allusions of I 4.13 ff,, a passage rich in Old Testament imagery, they would find it no more difficult to cope with the eschatological symbolism of II Thess.

(c) The problem raised in I 4.13 ff. is dependent upon the unexpected deaths of some of the church members. This would not necessarily have been the subject of instruction during the mission, whereas Antichrist might very well have been.

(d) This is the most cogent objection and does seem to suggest that someone—presumably a later writer—had written a letter in imitation of the apostle's style. In reply, it may be pointed out that two short letters dealing with the same subject, and written to the same people within a few weeks, are bound to betray close resemblances. If we deduct greetings, salutations and thanksgivings—which are part of the normal pattern of letters of the time—the parallelism amounts to no more than a third of the two epistles. Further, Paul may well have read over his first letter again before composing the second.

THE TRADITIONAL VIEW

But it is largely because scholars have felt that this similarity between the two epistles is difficult to understand that it has been suggested that the second letter is a forgery, or that it was written by Timothy or Silvanus. Other scholars, while admitting that both letters are from the same hand, have suggested that the first letter was written to Gentile Christians and the second letter to Jewish Christians, or that the first letter was intended for private circulation and the second for public reading in church. It can be seen from these varying suggestions that no single solution commands general agreement. Most scholars are now of the opinion that, while these minor problems should be faced, most of them can be answered satisfactorily, and no solution is as adequate as the traditional view that Paul is the author of both epistles.

WHERE AND WHEN?

The place of writing can be established without difficulty as Corinth. St Luke tells us that after the Macedonian campaign Paul was rejoined there by Silvanus and Timothy (Acts 18.5) and Paul himself tells us that it was at that point that he wrote the first letter (I 3.6). The second letter gives every indication of having been written only a short time later than the first while Paul was still in Corinth, where he spent eighteen months. The approximate date is likewise relatively easily established. An inscription found at Delphi indicates that Gallio (Acts 18.12) became proconsul of Achaia in A.D. 51. Since the practice was that Roman officials set out for new colonial appointments at the beginning of June, Gallio would arrive in Corinth about a month later. When Paul was haled before him the narrative implies that Gallio had just arrived, and that Paul had already been almost eighteen months in the city (Acts 18.11, 18). The apostle therefore probably reached Corinth at the beginning of A.D. 50. The Thessalonian campaign can therefore be dated as having taken place in the late autumn of 49 and the first letter to Thessalonica would be written early in 50, with the second letter following shortly afterwards. It is generally held that the Thessalonian letters were the first to be written by the apostle, though some scholars now believe that the epistle to the Galatians was written earlier.

COMMENTARY

THE FIRST EPISTLE
TO THE THESSALONIANS

I

THANKS BE TO GOD
1.1-10

A FRIENDLY GREETING
1.1

It is quite clear from all that follows in this letter that
Paul's relationship with the Thessalonian church was an
extremely friendly one. The success of the mission, of
which he had just learned (3.6), the impact which the little
community was having on its pagan environment, and the
assurance that the methods of presenting the gospel which
had been so successful in the vastly different milieu of the
Middle East were proving equally effective among the
Macedonians, were matters for profound thankfulness. The
opening words reflect the state of his mind. In Paul's day
the normal way to begin a letter was to start with the
writer's name, followed by the name of the recipient, and
then to add some words of greeting. Paul adheres to this
practice, but in most of the letters he sent which are still
preserved for us in the New Testament, he adds a
description of himself as an apostle or servant of Jesus
Christ.

FATHER IN GOD

He seems to have regarded this as an official title, to be
used in cases where his authority was questioned. Parti-
cularly in the letter to the Galatian church, where, as we
know, attempts were being made to discredit him on the

grounds that he was not one of the original apostolic band, he asserts at length in his opening greeting his claim to speak with the authority of one who had been directly commissioned by Christ (Gal. 1.1). But in this letter to the Thessalonians, as in his letter to Philemon, and in writing to the church at Philippi for which he had a special affection, he omits his official title. In all three cases he is addressing friends who have no need to be reminded of his status. No one questions his right to speak to them as their father in God.

SILVANUS AND TIMOTHY

Silvanus and Timothy are included in the greeting not because they are joint authors of the letter, but because they had had so much to do with the Thessalonian church. SILVANUS is the Silas of the Book of Acts who was Paul's companion on his second missionary journey which included the founding of a Christian community at Thessalonica (Acts 17.4, 10). TIMOTHY, a younger man, had joined the two evangelists at Lystra, and was likewise present during the Macedonian campaign (Acts 16.1-3). When Paul went on to Athens, Silvanus and Timothy had been left in Macedonia to follow up the mission there, and had later rejoined their leader at Corinth (see note on 3.1 ff). It was the good news which they brought of the effects of the Macedonian mission, as well as some problems that required an answer, which prompted this letter. Since they were with Paul when he wrote it, the triple greeting is only natural. It is equally understandable that he should write this and the following letter to Thessalonica as a joint message. The use of the plural throughout is not a literary convention. But it is of course the mind of Paul that is responsible for the contents of both epistles.

THE CHURCH

Paul was in all probability writing to a relatively small and unimportant group of Christians, meeting in the house of one of the members, perhaps Jason (Acts 17.5-9). The revival of the house-church in our own day is not just a practical attempt to overcome the problem of the church-less, it is a recovery of the earliest form of Christian worship. But Paul puts this house-meeting at Thessalonica into its proper perspective by calling it a CHURCH. The Church is not a mere gathering of like-minded individuals who have a fancy for singing hymns, as it is sometimes thought to be, but the Body of Christ, the living fellowship of Christ and his people, committed to the service of God and of one another. Of this divinely constituted society the little group of Thessalonians formed a part. They were no isolated outpost but integral members of God's Common-wealth, as significant in his sight as the great Christian com-munities of Antioch or Jerusalem.

THE PEOPLE OF GOD

The New Testament Greek word for ' church ' is *ekklesia*, the word which had been used in Old Testament times by Greek-speaking Jews to denote Israel in its religious aspect. When the early Christians, in imitation of Jesus, used this word to describe themselves, they were stressing their continuity with the vocation of Israel to be the People of God. Israel had failed, but a New Israel, heir to its mission and its rich spiritual legacy, had now taken its place. The *ekklesia* was the chosen instrument of God to recreate the world, to bring it into the right relationship with himself. This tiny handful of Macedonian Christians was thus caught up into a breath-taking union with Abraham and the saints of Old Testament times, with the growing number of men and women who had pledged their allegi-

C

ance to Christ in response to the challenge of Paul and his
fellow apostles, with those, as they will be told later (5.10),
who have finished the course and kept the faith, and most of
all with the living presence of the Head of the Body, Christ
himself. We often tend to forget that this is equally true of
every local congregation to-day, even the rather depressing
ones. They, too, are part of the New Humanity which
acknowledges God as FATHER and Jesus Christ as LORD.

GRACE

Perhaps because they are so familiar in other connections
the little one-syllable words in the Christian vocabulary
tend to be used more casually than the more ponderous
polysyllables which smack of high theology. Love and
faith, grace and peace, are, however, words of the deepest
significance in Christian thought. St. Paul certainly does not
employ them casually. When he uses this formula of
greeting—which is repeated with variations throughout his
letters—he is choosing his words carefully. The ordinary
Greek word for ' Greeting! ' which stood at the head of a
normal letter was *chairein*. The word for GRACE is *charis*.
Christianity takes the everyday word for greeting and trans-
forms it into the distinctive message of God's forgiving love
towards all men in Christ, which the word for GRACE
conveys.

PEACE

Similarly the usual Old Testament greeting was ' Peace! '
The Hebrew word *shalom* has its modern equivalent in the
mechanical *Salaam!* of the Middle East. Once more
Christianity infuses into the casual greeting the whole significance of the new relationship with God and the world
which Christ has made possible. East and West, Jew and
Greek, are here as so often in Christianity brought into a

new union which enriches both. Whether Paul originated this greeting or whether it was a common liturgical formula before his day, no two words could better express the essence of the difference that Christ makes to men's lives. Paul, Silvanus and Timothy could wish for no richer blessing for their Thessalonian friends than that they should experience the grace of the Lord Jesus Christ and the peace of God that passes all understanding.

PAUL GIVES THANKS TO GOD
1.2-10

It is characteristic both of the apostle and of this letter that the first note to be struck after the opening words of greeting is one of thanksgiving. Not only does this reflect Paul's instinctive response to good news, in that his first thought is to give God the glory, but also it is the measure of how much cause there was for thankfulness. That anyone at all should be found in the idol-infested, sex-ridden atmosphere of a pagan city to listen to the gospel of the crucified and risen Carpenter was astonishing enough, but when in fact the preaching of the missionaries had stirred the hearts of enough people to make the Christian community of Thessalonica a talking point far beyond the city, this was surely the hand of God at work in no uncertain manner.

MEN OF PRAYER

The three missionaries were all men of prayer in the widest sense of the word. The concerns of their fellow Christians were their concerns. The fervent faith and brotherly charity of the new converts were as rightly a matter for thanksgiving to God, as their afflictions and anxieties were cause for intercession on their behalf. The

apostles speak of praying ALWAYS and WITHOUT CEASING.
This should not be taken as a pious exaggeration. No men
could have achieved what these early messengers of Christ
accomplished if they had not been men whose whole lives
were built on constant communion with God. In this they
followed in the footsteps of their Master. Further, when
they prayed for the Thessalonians it was not only for their
special friends, as most of us tend to do, but for them ALL
—and there is no reason to suppose that the Thessalonian
church consisted of any less odd a collection of characters
than the average congregation to-day. But the missionaries
thanked God for them all and prayed for them all, as men
and women for whom Christ had died.

FAITH, HOPE AND LOVE
1.3

Faith, hope and love are rightly regarded as the three
distinctively Christian virtues. St Paul refers to them frequently, and above all in the great hymn of I Cor. 13. Each
of them expresses an essential element of Christian belief
and practice. It is unlikely that Paul was originally responsible for their association. They were probably from the
earliest days of the Christian mission regarded as the hall-
mark of Christian witness. FAITH expressed a personal
relationship of trust and dependence, a commitment of the
whole personality to God as we know him in Jesus Christ.
It is our response to God's grace. Christian HOPE is the
reverse of any fatalistic belief in the cyclical nature of
history, or in blind chance, or in the nothingness which
breeds despair. It affirms the conviction that the reins of
history are in God's hands and that the end of everything
will be God's victory, in which the ordinary Christian
shares. Christian LOVE has little to do with the bastardized
use of the word to-day as a synonym for lust. It means

selfless caring, the readiness to give oneself without thought
of reward in the service of God and one's neighbour.

All three of these Christian attitudes are bound to issue
in action. Christianity can never be defined solely in terms
of an attitude. It involves that certainly—what we believe
is basically important. But it must issue in what we do and
in how we do it. In the case of the Thessalonians to whom
Paul is writing, their FAITH and LOVE had resulted in works
of self-denial and costly self-giving, just as their Christian
HOPE had enabled them to endure opposition. All three
virtues and their sequel in action sprang from a right
relationship to God which had been made possible through
Christ.

MEN WHOM GOD HAS CHOSEN
1.4-5

Paul's knowledge of the Thessalonian church is no hear-
say. He had lived among them and had seen for himself
how they had responded to the appeal of the missionaries.
Their ready acceptance of the gospel and the change that
took place in their lives were clear proof that God had
touched their hearts. It was neither the preaching of the
evangelists nor the efforts of the converts that had brought
this about. It was God's choice of them to be his witnesses
and servants and his power alone that had enabled them
to answer his call. This is what Paul means by their
ELECTION. Perhaps the experience was vividly in his mind
of his early days at Corinth, from where he was writing
this letter, and where to all accounts he was very unsure
of his ground. Physically a sick man and smarting from his
rebuff at Athens, his first campaign in Corinth lacked fire
and sparkle (I Cor. 2.3).

It was all the greater contrast, therefore, to think back
to the exhilarating days of the Thessalonian mission. The

apostles had been conscious that their preaching was no
ordinary preaching on that occasion. They had felt that in
some strange and powerful compulsion the Spirit of God
had seized hold of them and given their words unwonted
weight and themselves unusual confidence. They too had
been caught up and, as it were, swept off their feet by a
mighty manifestation of what God could do, when both
preachers and hearers surrendered themselves wholly to
him. In the next chapter Paul goes on to say something
more of the effect the mission had on the apostles themselves.

IMITÁTIO CHRISTI
1.6

It is a commonplace that the strongest argument against
Christianity is not theological or philosophical or scientific
but practical—the abysmal failure of Christians to behave
like Christians. All our preaching and teaching, our
reasoned defences of the faith and passionate advocacy of
the truth are so much hot air if our lives are indistinguishable from those to whom the Cross is foolishness. If we
are less tolerant and charitable, less generous and unselfish,
less patient and humble, than those who have ' no time for
the Church' we cannot be surprised if they are confirmed
in their apathy.

No one could accuse Paul of pagan pride when he speaks
here of the Thessalonians having become IMITATORS of
Christ by taking the apostles as their model. Paul was too
great a soul, too suffused with the spirit of Christ to take
any credit for what he was. But the evidence of history is
that he was changed from being a venomous, bigoted and
cruel persecutor of helpless men and women to one who
faced death not once but many times for his Master's sake,
who spent himself night and day in the service of others,

and who was loved as only one could be loved who lived the Christ-life.

VIA DOLOROSA

He and his fellow missionaries had come to Thessalonica with a new message, but they had backed it with the irrefutable evidence of their own transformed personalities. They proved the truth of the gospel by their own witness. And as is the case with missionaries in the foreign field to-day their converts learned to follow in the footsteps of Christ by placing their feet in the prints that their teachers had made. It was from them that they learned above all how to tread the path of suffering, how to endure the uncomprehending antagonism of their pagan neighbours, to say nothing of the more violent hostility which became their constant companion as it was of Paul and his associates. But in learning from them how to meet it through an ever deeper trust and reliance on the power of God, which turned their afflictions into joy, they were treading at the same time the Via Dolorosa which Christ himself had trodden.

THE LORD'S TRUMPET
1.7-8

Looking back over the events which led to the Thessalonian campaign, Paul could not help but see divine guidance behind them. He had wanted to spread the gospel in the provinces of Asia and Bithynia but something had prevented him (Acts 16.6-7). It may have been local Jewish opposition or official obstructionism. We cannot now tell. At all events he found himself at Troas, a seaport which seemed to offer no prospects at all for his evangelical zeal. But it was there that he had his dream of the man from

Macedonia, perhaps St Luke, as Ramsay suggested, and
in response to it had crossed the straits into what is now
the continent of Europe. There followed the founding of
the churches of Philippi and Thessalonica—both of which
were to occupy a special place in the apostle's affection. In
particular the response at Thessalonica seems to have been
instantaneous and startling. Little wonder that Paul saw
the frustration of his earlier plans to have been the work
of the Spirit, directing him from what he wanted to do to
what God wanted him to do.

NO NINE DAYS' WONDER

It is in this light that we should regard his unbounded
thankfulness and joy over every evidence that his Macedonian campaign had been in fact divinely inspired. What
Silvanus and Timothy had now told him only confirmed
what he had himself sensed at the time. But as a wiser man
than many of us Paul knew better than to rely entirely on
the inward glow of fervour and the instantaneous response.
The question was: Would it last? This was what he did not
know until the other two apostles came to Corinth. From
them however he had learned that the mission, far from
being a flash in the pan, had resulted in a transformation
of life and character among the Thessalonians which was
being talked about far beyond their own city. They had set
an example of loyalty to Christ, of steadfastness in face of
persecution, and of brotherly charity, which was a model
to all other Christians not only in their own province of
MACEDONIA but southwards into ACHAIA and even beyond.

Paul speaks of their witness as a clarion call to the rest
of the world. Their example of faith had become a
summons to others, as if God were proclaiming through
them the truth of the saving power of Christ so that all
mankind should hear. If we think of the constant traffic
that went on in the ancient world, along the great Roman

roads, and of the importance of Thessalonica as a commercial centre, it is not difficult to imagine how tales of a
new kind of religious movement would be carried by
merchants and travellers, or with what delight such news
would be passed on by any Christian who came to hear
of it.

FROM IDOLATRY TO FAITH
1.9

Such was the impression that the recent events in Thessalonica had made that the apostles were spared the necessity
of talking about it themselves. People came to tell *them*
about it! The story of their arrival was common knowledge,
as was the welcome they received. But it was the sequel
that mattered most, the dramatic renunciation of pagan
idolatry for the service of the TRUE GOD. Paul's normal
practice on arriving in an unfamiliar city was to establish
contact with the Jewish community. This 'Hebrew of the
Hebrews' had, despite his consciousness that he had been
called to be the apostle of the Gentiles, an intense conviction that the Jews stood in a special relationship to God
which even their rejection of Jesus as the Messiah could
not alter. They had been chosen to be God's people. It was
to them that God had revealed his will and purpose and it
was as a Jew that he had sent his Son. They were therefore
an integral part of the Kingdom. They must be won for
Christ and as Christ had preached the gospel to them so
must his followers give them first place in their missionary
activities. Accordingly it was to the local synagogue that
Paul invariably turned his steps in any new city, and
sometimes his message fell on responsive ears.

But he had a more ready response from such devout
pagans as had attached themselves to the synagogues as
adherents: men and women who found in the Law and

Prophecy of the Jews an austere discipline and an oasis of stability in a world empty alike of moral standards and religious conviction. These people had already set their feet upon the path that led through the God of the Old Testament to a ready acceptance of his final revelation of himself in his Son.

WHAT IT MEANT TO BE A PAGAN

It is clear from Paul's words here, however, that the Thessalonian church had not been recruited from Jews or God-fearing pagans of this character, but from out-and-out heathenism. It was this fact that made the success of the mission so dramatic, and its sequel in the witness of changed lives so outstanding. Let us have no illusions about what it meant to be a pagan. There were no wide-eyed simple children of nature in these imperial cities who cherished an innocent faith in the stately pantheon of ancient Greece or Rome. The Stoics and other philosophers made some impact on the educated section of society and in these circles a high ethical standard was observed. But for the ordinary man and woman, bewildered by a multiplicity of temples and shrines to innumerable gods and goddesses, astrology and demonology provided the normal background to life. Eroticism was synonymous with worship. Expediency dictated behaviour. Life was a gamble with fate and ended in extinction. For Paul the miracle of Thessalonica was that it was men and women whose attitude to life was one of amoral fatalism, against a background of sensuous polytheism, who had turned from that to serve the true and living God in the fellowship of the Risen Christ.

IN THE SHADOW OF THE JUDGMENT
1.10

The LIVING God whom Paul proclaimed was not merely an animate Being as opposed to blocks of wood and stone but, as the whole of the Old Testament declares and the New Testament confirms, a God who is active in the affairs of the world and in the lives of men, who demands moral obedience from societies and individuals, who condemns sin although he forgives the repentant sinner. Paul's words here reflect the earliest form of the preaching of the gospel as we find it in the sermon-summaries in the Book of Acts. Later his own rich and creative mind was to restate it in the more characteristic language of the later epistles, in terms of justification by faith, reconciliation with God, and life in Christ. The language here is more that of the tradition which Paul himself received, but the theology is essentially the same. It is the good news that God cared so much for men and women that he sent his Son among them to defeat evil and death and to gather them to himself in a new fellowship of love and service in which they are delivered from the consequences of their own sin and folly to share life eternal with him.

LIVING IN TWO WORLDS

In all its history the Church has regarded itself as being already in a New Age. The old order came to an end with the advent of Jesus, an order in which sin and death reigned supreme. With his coming a foretaste of the perfect Rule of God came into the world. Men and women who respond to his summons step out of the old order into the new, and become partakers of the life of the Age to Come. They are in the world but not entirely of it. Their goings and comings are on the same plane as those of their neighbours but their real lives are hid with Christ in God. They are citizens of two kingdoms—the kingdom of this world and the kingdom of God. In times of intense religious fervour, as in the early Church and during periods of revival, this sense of belonging already to the Age to Come is experienced in acute form. It is as if this old imperfect world were about to disappear and the new age of God were on the point of being ushered in. It seemed to the earliest believers, living as they did in a hostile world, and being intensely aware of the proximity of the world beyond, that at any moment the old evil order would be swept away and the new age of Christ would supervene, heralded by his return.

THE SECOND ADVENT

God had sent his Son. While a few had followed him during his earthly ministry the vast majority had rejected him. God had however proved them to be wrong by raising his Son from the dead. The evil machinations of men and the demonic forces that brought about disease and death alike had no power over him. But while his followers knew this and knew moreover that the Risen Christ was now with the Father, the world at large did not as yet acknowledge it, and still pursued its evil ways unchecked. This could not be for long. There must be final and clear proof on the world's stage that God's rule was supreme, that sin and evil had had their day, and that Christ was indeed Victor over all his foes. Messiah must return, not as the humble Carpenter to be done to death upon a Cross, but as the Triumphant King and Lord of all, Judge of all the nations, to reward virtue and punish vice.

THE TRIUMPH OF CHRIST

There were many reasons why this sense of the impending end of the world and a second Advent should have been so strong—Jesus' own words seemed to lend colour to such a belief, as did the extraordinary atmosphere of the Church following the Resurrection and Pentecost, the mighty works done by the apostles and the spectacular spread of the gospel with its life-changing power. Was not this what the prophets had foretold would happen when the Messianic Age began? This then was the message that had been proclaimed to the Thessalonians, as in all other missionary campaigns. This evil world stood under the Judgment of God: injustice, corruption, cruelty and perversion would reap their deserts. The only hope for men and women involved in such a society was to step out of it into the new society which the mercy of God had made possible. By turning their backs on the past and committing their lives to Christ in this fellowship of the redeemed they could calmly await the none too distant day when Christ would return to claim his own and the New Age in all its fulness would begin. Behind this early conviction of a speedy and visible return of Christ to the world that he had so recently left, we should not fail to recognize the essential emphasis that in God's good time the Triumph of Christ and his Cause is assured. This is shown by the fact that when Christ did not return as they expected the faith of the early Christians was in no way shaken.

PAUL DEFENDS HIS RECORD
2.1-16

It might seem odd that such a passage as now follows should be necessary at all in a letter so clearly reflecting the utmost confidence and affection between the writer and the readers. Immediately following the words of commendation in the last chapter it is surprising to find Paul suddenly launching into a detailed apology for his own behaviour and that of his fellow missionaries during their campaign in Thessalonica. The explanation is simple and the clue is to be found in v. 15. There were no disaffected members in the Thessalonian community, no pockets of resistance to apostolic authority, no scandals requiring correction, but there was a sustained and vitriolic attack upon the Christian missionaries and upon Paul in particular which was being carried out by the local Jews there as in every other part of Paul's missionary province.

IMPLACABLE ENEMIES

If Paul had cause to complain of the hesitancy and conservatism of his Christian colleagues in Jerusalem in their desire to placate the local Jews, he had much more cause to feel that outside Palestine no amount of placation would make any difference to the fanatical hatred of many of his countrymen towards Christianity and himself as its chief protagonist. He was regarded as a traitor to Judaism, a perverter of the truth that had been delivered in the Law and the Prophets. The savage attacks of these overseas

Jews pursued him on his travels and ultimately brought
about his arrest and imprisonment (Acts 21.27 ff.). It was
the local Jews in Thessalonica who had brought the mission
there to an abrupt end, and had followed the apostles to
Beroea with the same result (Acts 17.5, 13).

It appears from this chapter that their hostility had not
abated once they had got rid of their chief enemy, but that
since the visit of the apostles they had been conducting a
campaign of vilification, imputing the basest motives to
Paul and his associates, accusing them of being little better
than itinerant religious quacks. These attacks, no doubt
reported to Paul at Corinth by Timothy on his visit, must
have been sufficiently serious for the apostle to have to
defend himself so strongly against them as he does here.
Obviously he did not underrate the unconscious effect of
lying propaganda on the minds of even his most loyal
supporters.

MUCH CONFLICT
2.1-2

Paul begins this new section of his letter by picking up
the thread of his remarks in 1.9, where he had referred to
the original visit of the apostles to Thessalonica, a visit
which, as he had reminded his readers earlier, had been
signalized by its remarkable effect on both preachers and
hearers (1.5). No one could gainsay the reality of the
spiritual awakening or the integrity of the apostles who
were the instruments of its appearance.

They had arrived in Thessalonica still smarting from the
ill-treatment and indignities they had received at Philippi.
There, according to the narrative of Acts 16.12 ff., they had
aroused the ire of the owners of a slave-girl by depriving
her of her psychic powers and her masters of the revenue
which accrued from her superstitious clients. The upshot

was a public flogging and imprisonment. Undaunted by these experiences, however, the apostles proceeded straight to Thessalonica and opened their mission there, prepared to face similar treatment, if need be, for the sake of the gospel. Men who could sing psalms at midnight in a prison dungeon after a typical Roman flogging were not to be easily deterred. The God who had led them thus far through all their trials would protect them still. Although the mission was conducted amid great CONFLICT, which most likely means Jewish opposition, the apostles persisted in their work.

SLANDEROUS CHARGES
2.3

It is clear from the expressions which Paul uses in his self-defence that the Jews who were trying to discredit him were not mincing their words. They were accusing him of being a crazy, lecherous religious fraud. There were so many in those days whom this description fitted that it is not so fantastic a charge as a similar calumny uttered now-adays about a missionary would be. Paul at all events takes it seriously and rightly so. The Roman Empire had within its bounds every possible variation in religion that could result from the blending of exotic oriental faiths with the by-products of Greek philosophy. Dabblers in the occult, pedlars of black magic, cranks and charlatans competed with serious and disinterested sponsors of new religious cults and austere philosophies. It was only too easy to discredit an honest exponent of new ideas by identifying him with the riff-raff of ' holy men ' and purveyors of bogus nostrums who battened on the credulous crowds in the market-places of the great cities.

ERROR

The R.V. text disguises the radical nature of the slanders that were being talked about the apostles. The three words ERROR, UNCLEANNESS and GUILE represent grave charges. They imply that the gospel message, which the Thessalonians had welcomed, was crazy nonsense invented by men of no principles whose only concern was to feather their own nests. It is not difficult to see how libellous accusations of this kind could arise in the first instance and in time sow seeds of doubt in the minds of the Thessalonian converts. After all on the face of it to both Jews and Greeks the Christian message of the Resurrection was hard to swallow. The Jews could believe in a Messiah and a Judgment, but not in a crucified Messiah and a risen Jesus of Nazareth. To most pagan minds any idea of one true and living God who held men accountable for their actions was sufficiently unattractive and uncomfortable to ensure that it would be dismissed at once as rubbish. The fact that some of the inhabitants of Thessalonica had been persuaded that the apostles' message was in fact the only true one among the multiplicity of creeds and systems of philosophy which clamoured for their attention was no guarantee that they would always remain impervious to any suggestion that Christianity was any less of a delusion than its rivals.

UNCLEANNESS

One of the favourite charges levelled against the early Christians was that of sexual promiscuity. Certainly some of their practices appeared to lend colour to this accusation. Their characteristic meeting was known as the ' love-feast ', at which they exchanged the kiss of peace. Men and women who were unmarried lived together as brother and sister (I Cor. 7.36 ff.) and the secrecy with which they were forced

D

to shroud their meetings in time of persecution gave added
weight to the suggestion that under cover of darkness—
especially in the catacombs of Rome—nameless orgies were
indulged in. The pagans could take little exception to this.
Sacramental fornication was part of the worship of many
of their cults. Paul's letters to the Corinthians and to the
Romans shed a revealing light upon the sex-laden atmosphere of the Gentile world. But the Jews, whose besetting
sins were rather those of the spirit than of the flesh, found
this insinuation that sexual morality among the Christians
was at least no better than that of their pagan rivals, a
useful weapon in their campaign of discrediting the new
faith. Paul simply rejects this charge as if it were unworthy
of a stated defence.

GUILE

The third accusation against the apostles was that of
being indistinguishable from any other money-making
street-corner orators who wheedle a living from gullible
bystanders. Men who came to Thessalonica as apostles of
a Master who had done 'mighty works', of a faith which
claimed to heal men's bodies as well as their souls, and of
a Spirit which moved men to speak with tongues, laid themselves open to the suggestion that they were purveyors of
black magic rather than of salvation, and that there was
little to choose between their variety and that of sorcerers
like Elymas (Acts 13.8 ff.) and Simon (Acts 8.9 ff.) who
made their living by exploiting the credulity of the
populace.

PAUL'S ANSWER
2.4-8

Before proceeding to a detailed defence of his conduct

while at Thessalonica Paul states what is in effect the basic
reason why charges of this sort are so fantastic as to require
no answer. The apostles are not casual dabblers in a new
religious faith but men who have been sifted and tested by
God and thereafter chosen by God to act as his messengers.
Paul had a profound sense of his own vocation and of the
part he had been called to play in spreading the gospel.
But here his argument is that all three of the apostles had
been entrusted with the proclamation of the Good News
only because they were called to the task by the one LIVING
AND TRUE GOD. As his servants it would be out of the
question for them to adopt the tactics of the average
religious charlatan. They were not concerned with what
men thought about them but only with their obligations to
God. God is their sole judge.

FALSE CHARGES

Behind the words of vv. 5-6 are obviously three specific
accusations directed against the behaviour of the apostles
during the mission. The charge of using FLATTERY is not
so much that of fawning over their audiences, as that of
gaining their confidence by smooth-tongued oratory like
present day vendors of patent medicines in street markets.
These were the tactics of the vagrant rhetoricians, whose
object was mainly financial. This leads naturally to the
second charge, which is that the apostles' real motive was
their private gain. A CLOKE OF COVETOUSNESS might cover
any personal ambition in high sounding moral principles.
Thirdly, says the apostle, God knows we did not seek any
GLORY OF MEN. Neither their converts nor anyone else
could accuse them of having sought to divert attention from
the substance of their message and attract it to themselves.
They came as servants of Christ, as no more than the
channel through which the word of salvation might reach
others. Yet as Paul rightly adds they might well have in-

sisted on being treated as men of some consequence since
they were Christ's commissioned representatives. The word
which the R.V. translates as BURDENSOME might mean that
the apostles could, if they had wished, legitimately have
expected to be supported financially by the Thessalonian
converts. It could also mean, and this is more probable,
that they could have stood on their dignity as special
messengers of Christ (see R.V. margin).

But this they certainly had not done. On the contrary,
says Paul, the relationship was far more like that between
a NURSE and the CHILDREN given into her care. There is a
variant reading in v. 7 (see R.V. margin) which makes little
difference either way. Most MSS. have the word *nepioi*
which means 'infants' where the R.V. reads *epioi* meaning
GENTLE. So great indeed was our affection for you, continues Paul, that we not only gave you the glorious gospel
message but all that we could give of ourselves—our love
and service.

HARD FACTS
2.9-11

Whatever suggestions of self-interested motives on the
part of the apostles may have been put about by their
opponents, there were certain facts in the record of the
mission at Thessalonica which were inescapable. The chief
fact was that throughout the campaign the apostles had
even refused to accept hospitality from anyone, far less
sums of money, but had supported themselves by taking
jobs, including a large amount of overtime judged by
present day standards, and by fitting in their preaching and
teaching in what time was left for leisure. This was so unlike the practice of the normal run of itinerant 'holy men'
and philosophers that Paul rightly lays great stress on it as
the surest proof of his integrity.

WORK AND WORSHIP

This was not the only occasion when Paul drew attention to the fact that none of his opponents could ever accuse him of sponging on his converts (I Cor. 4.12). In his address to the elders of the church at Ephesus he even suggested that he had worked to support his colleagues as well (Acts 20.33-35). We are told that Paul was by trade a tentmaker (Acts 18.3). This was in accordance with the Jewish regulation that every boy, even if he were destined to follow a professional career, should first have been apprenticed to some craft. Paul's brilliant mind had obviously earmarked him for a career as a rabbi, but despite this, and the fact that his father as a freeman of the Roman Empire was probably well-to-do, he had been trained in a trade which played a prominent part in the economy of his native city of Tarsus. Whatever he earned by the sweat of his brow at Thessalonica, it does not seem to have been enough for his needs, although 'needs' in the case of Paul probably meant a good deal more than providing for his own maintenance. In his letter to Philippi he refers to gifts of money which he had received from there during the Thessalonian campaign (Phil. 4.16). His main point however is to refute the allegation that there was any Thessalonian money involved, although some of the Christian converts could probably have afforded a contribution (Acts 17.4).

BY THEIR FRUITS YE SHALL KNOW THEM

The second hard fact that the apostle adduces is the conduct of the missionaries. If they were merely the type of smooth-tongued charlatans who normally frequented the market-place, as their calumniators suggested, did their behaviour during the mission support the charge? Had their attitude towards the converts not been wholly in harmony with their message? As they well remembered,

the missionaries had not only exhibited integrity of character, being 'honest, straightforward and above criticism'
(Phillips), but had treated the members of the little church
as if they had been their own children, giving each one of
them the advice and help and affection that a good father
gives to his sons.

THE KINGDOM AND THE GLORY
2.12

And all this, continues Paul, the physical toil and the
loving service alike, was for one purpose only, that others
should be brought into the new life which the missionaries
themselves had come to know. This 'God-intoxication' of
the apostle, as it has been called, makes him subordinate
everything to this one aim, to bring as many others as he
could to the point of encounter with God; to lead them to
the moment when they stood face to face with the Father
who was summoning them into his service. In Paul's view
the purpose of his preaching was to enable men to hear
God's call. Once they responded, the whole meaning of
their lives from then on consisted in living in such a way
as to be worthy of the God who had called them.

TWICE-BORN

As is indicated in the R.V. margin some of the Greek
MSS have the word 'called' in the past tense, where the
R.V. prefers the present tense. Either reading would be significant, but the R.V. CALLETH has a wider sense. God's call
to us, Paul is saying, is both a definite moment in time
and a renewed experience. There was a time when God
called each one of us into his service. For some, as in the
case of Paul himself, it is an easily remembered day and
hour. On the Damascus road the old cruel bigoted Rabbi

Saul died and a new man in Christ was born. The Thessalonians likewise could look back on the time when God called them through the preaching of the gospel by the apostles.

DAILY RE-BIRTH

In most cases of those who have been brought up in the Christian Church and in a Christian home no such dramatic event signals the change. But God has called us. It may be at confirmation, it may be at adult baptism, or at marriage, or with the added responsibility of a family. If we have committed our lives to God and the service of his Church we can look back at least to a time when these things did not have for us the significance they have now. There is, then, a time of calling in each of our lives. But Paul goes further and reminds us that this is not only a once and for all event, but that God is constantly calling us back into his service, and needs to call us, even when we are already committed to him, if we are to WALK WORTHILY of him.

LIFE IN CHRIST

In so far as our lives are lived in the right relationship to God we are already in his KINGDOM. The kingdom or realm of God is where his will is done. We are made citizens of the kingdom at our baptism and by the grace of God in response to his continuous call we grow in understanding and perception of his will, so that our citizenship becomes more than a nominal enrolment. But as always with Paul it is the end result that he has in mind. We are not simply called to live under the rule of God in the world as we know it, but to share in the fulness of the life of the Age to Come, when God's sovereignty is acknowledged by all and over all. Just as the full realization of the kingdom lies beyond this present age, so does our vision of his

GLORY. As Paul says elsewhere (I Cor. 13.12), here we see
the reflection, but there we shall see face to face. As citizens
of the kingdom, in so far as we live in the company of
Christ, we see as much of the glory of God as the human
mind can comprehend. But the promise is that the fulfilment of our calling is to experience the unutterable splen-
dour of his eternal presence.

PAUL AND THE JEWS
2.13-16

Some commentators take the view that this passage that
follows is not entirely from Paul's pen. It begins in a mood
of congratulation of the Thessalonian Church, which is in
harmony with what has gone before, but develops into a
denunciation of the Jews which is sharper in tone than anything else in the Pauline epistles and does not seem to
square with Paul's conception of his countrymen as in a
peculiar sense still the Chosen People despite their failure
to acknowledge Jesus as the Messiah (cf. Rom. 9-11).

A MOOD OF THE MOMENT

On the other hand it is difficult to know where Paul
stops and the interpolator begins. It may be that the second
half of verse 16 is the pious comment of some early copyist
but as it stands it appears to provide a fitting climax to the
argument. Certainly it is an impassioned outburst of
indignation against the Jews which is more vehement than
it might be. But is it any more so than the circumstances
call for? Paul's letters often give the impression of being
dashed off in the heat of the campaign, to deal with some
particular problem, to bestow praise or administer a
rebuke. They are not in general the products of prolonged
and careful composition. It would seem to be quite in

keeping with this that they should occasionally reflect the mood of a moment rather than a considered point of view. There is no compelling reason why we should regard this passage as anything other than pardonable apostolic exasperation.

NO MAN-MADE PHILOSOPHY

The apostle, continuing his recollection of the mission campaign, recalls with gratitude to God that the preaching of the missionaries was from the start regarded by the Thessalonians as a word from God and not as a man-made philosophy of life. Its effect upon them had shown that they had been right to do so, for no human philosophy could have sustained them in the persecution which they had suffered since they accepted the gospel. Just as the Christian communities in Palestine had had to endure violence from their compatriots, so the Thessalonian Christians in their turn had been at the mercy of the pagan neighbours whose beliefs they no longer shared. They were thus bound in a fellowship of suffering with their Jewish Christian brethren.

VENDETTA

But the mention of Jewish persecution seems to spark off an outburst of resentment in the apostle's mind. Although it was the Gentile rabble at Thessalonica which had brought the mission to an abrupt end, the local Jews had been the instigators. Their vindictiveness had pursued Paul to Beroea, and once more in Corinth, from where he was writing, the same violent opposition was emerging. It appears from the narrative of the Book of Acts that the early stages of Paul's stay in Corinth had been relatively placid (Acts 18.1-4). As we have seen, the apostle was not in his usual form. But when Silvanus and Timothy arrived

from Macedonia with their welcome news and Paul
launched into his normal uncompromising presentation of
the gospel, the reaction on the part of the Jews seems to
have markedly changed for the worse. If, as he indicates in
3.6, this letter was written just at this point it would explain
the vigour of Paul's denunciation of the Jews as he saw
the familiar pattern again unfolding itself.

RELIGIOUS INTOLERANCE

These are the people, he bursts out passionately, who
killed our Lord, their own Messiah. They had done the
same to God's messengers, the prophets, in days gone by,
and they were doing their best to make life impossible for
Christ's messengers, the apostles. Paul had had to leave
Damascus because of them soon after his conversion to
Christianity (Acts 9.23 ff.) and their hatred had pursued
him ever since. When Tacitus at a later date accused the
Jews of being enemies of mankind he was unconsciously
echoing Paul's sentiments here. It may be that Tacitus himself was using a common pagan description of the Jews
and that Paul is in effect saying: Well may the world speak
of their hatred of the human race, for their crime is the
greatest sin of all, in that they prevent us from proclaiming
the message of salvation to the Gentiles. Tacitus, of course,
shared the same opinion about the Christians.

NATIONALISM AND MISSION

This had been the traditional besetting sin of Jewry.
They were the chosen People of God, destined to dominate
the Gentiles. The message of the prophets, from Amos
onwards, had been that God was the God of the Gentiles
as well as of the Jews. Second Isaiah and the writer of
Jonah had gone further and summoned them to a realization of their true vocation and the fulfilment of God's

purpose in bringing the Gentile world to the knowledge of
the true God. This they had steadfastly refused to do and
part of their violent hatred of Christianity was that this
was precisely the aim to which the Church was committed.
In their view, to by-pass the prescribed route through
Judaism was contrary to the will of God and they sought
to prevent it with all the strength of a religious fanaticism
which conceives vital theological principles to be at
stake.

THE JUDGMENT OF GOD

Paul rounds off his catalogue of the crimes of his countrymen with some trenchant words reminiscent of Old Testament prophecy. Indeed the metaphor he uses is found more
than once in the Old Testament (Ps. 11.6; Gen. 15.16). His
thought is that their latest attempt to thwart the purpose
of God is the last straw, or, in Biblical language, the last
drop in the cup of their deserts which they now must drink.
The metaphor of the cup is used both of blessing (e.g. Ps.
23.5) and of cursing. Here it is obviously the latter. By preventing the spread of the gospel, says the apostle, the Jews
have invited the ultimate Judgment of God.

BEYOND THE LAST CHANCE

The WRATH of God is the punishment they have brought
on themselves. They were given chance after chance, by
the prophets and finally by the Messiah, as our Lord indicated in the Parable of the Wicked Husbandmen (Mark
12.1 ff.). Even then the mercy of God offered them a
breathing-space, as Peter called it (Acts 3.19-21) in which
they had a last opportunity to repent of their obstinacy
and become part of the reconstituted Israel of God. Their
conduct in rejecting the gospel and persecuting the apostles
as they had done to the prophets and the Lord Jesus him-

self showed that they had forfeited their last chance. God's Judgment was about to fall upon his renegade people.

HISTORY AND THEOLOGY

There is little point in enquiring whether Paul had in mind the Fall of Jerusalem which was to take place twenty years later and which even then must have seemed to many the inevitable end of the gradually worsening relationship between the Jews and the Romans in Palestine. In the mind of the early Christians history and theology were inextricably woven together. Every act of retribution in which evil was recompensed was regarded as an act of God which fitted into the pattern of his inexorable justice. Doubtless in Paul's mind, as in any other Christian mind at that time, the WRATH or the Judgment was identified with the eschatological event which would wind up the present age and inaugurate the victorious Reign of Christ. But since God was Lord of all history, any event which conformed to the pattern of his Judgment was also interpreted as the work of his hands. Somehow, sometime, the Jews will get their deserts.

III

FOLLOW-UP TO THE MISSION
2.17–3.13

When we turn to v. 17 it seems at first sight as if Paul, having unburdened himself about the Jews, resumes his normal pastoral tone. But he is not finished with the Jews yet. He embarks now upon an account of what has happened at Corinth since the mission to Thessalonica, of how being unable to visit them himself he sent Timothy, of what news Timothy brought, and of its effect upon Paul This lasts until the end of chapter 3.

PAUL EXPLAINS HIS ABSENCE
2.17-20

Reading between the lines, however, it would seem likely that the reason why such a prolonged apology was necessary was that one of the insinuations being made by his Jewish detractors at Thessalonica was that this fine missionary had gone off and left them without wasting a further thought on them, doubtless to find another circle of equally gullible dupes in Corinth whom he could proceed to exploit. If in addition to this Paul had given a definite promise to return which he had not been able to fulfil, it is easy to see why he should emphasize this point so strongly.

I, PAUL

Paul's aim is therefore to assure the converts that

nothing would have given him more happiness than to come
back to Thessalonica. He had felt like a father bereaved
of his children. His friends had never been out of his
thoughts although they were far away. Time and again
he had tried to get back to them—and to emphasize it he
changes from his normal practice in this letter of associating
the names of Silvanus and Timothy with his name. I, PAUL,
not the other missionaries only, but I myself tried
desperately hard to return, despite what these scandalous
rumours say.

PREVENTED BY SATAN

But SATAN HINDERED us. Obviously Paul means to indicate by this something beyond his control and of an evil
character. The fact that he reverts to the plural US seems
to rule out any interpretation which would connect it with
his physical condition, his ' thorn in the flesh ', whether it
was malaria or epilepsy (II Cor. 12.7 ff.; Gal. 4.13). There
is no indication that Silvanus and Timothy were prevented
by illness. Further, when Paul on another occasion was
hindered from going where he wanted to go he attributed
it to divine agency—the Spirit of Jesus or the Holy Spirit
(Acts 16.6-7). In that case he seems to have regarded it as
providential guidance. This time however the use of SATAN,
implying diabolical agency, in close association with his
recent outburst against the Jews, would suggest some
machinations by Jewish opponents. The Thessalonians
probably had heard something about this from Timothy
(cf. 3.2) and the apostle does not need to explain it
further.

PAUL'S GLORY AND JOY

Then in a fine burst of affection, as if to clinch any
doubts they may have had about his lack of concern for

them, he asks them what greater JOY lies before him than
to present his Thessalonian brethren, now gathered into
the Christian fold, to the LORD JESUS himself at his appear-
ing. Once again (cf. 1.10) by reference to the *Parousia* or
Second Advent of Christ Paul emphasizes this cardinal
feature of the missionaries' message and prepares the way
for a more detailed treatment of the subject later in the
letter (see note on the Second Advent, pp. 83-94).

TIMOTHY'S VISIT TO THESSALONICA
3.1-5

The chapter division here seems to be dictated more by
a convenient splitting up of the text than by the sense.
From 2.17-3.10 Paul gives a continuous narrative, account-
ing for his failure to return to Thessalonica, followed by
his despatch of Timothy in his place, and his reaction to
the news Timothy brought back from Macedonia.

Being prevented from visiting his Thessalonian friends
Paul decided to send an ambassador. Two small difficulties
arise, neither of them insuperable, when we compare the
record of the missionaries' journeys in the Book of Acts
with what Paul says here. In Acts there is no mention of
Timothy being in Athens at all, and, secondly, there is the
question of whether Paul means to include Silvanus when
he says WE THOUGHT IT GOOD TO BE LEFT BEHIND AT ATHENS
ALONE.

Let us follow the account in Acts (17.10-14) first of all.
Paul, Silvanus and Timothy left Thessalonica hurriedly and
secretly after the riot instigated by the Jews. Their next campaign, apparently of short duration, was at Beroea, about
fifty miles to the south west. Pursued there by the Thessalonian Jews who had heard of their activities they found
themselves once more in trouble. Paul as the chief enemy
of the Jews was escorted safely out of the city to the coast,

where he took a ship for Athens. Silvanus and Timothy remained at Beroea.

PAUL IN ATHENS

Paul was accompanied to Athens by some of the Beroean converts, who returned at once to their home town, with an urgent message from Paul that Silvanus and Timothy should join him at once. It is generally thought that the necessity for an escort, coupled with the unexpected request that Silvanus and Timothy should join him, indicates that Paul was at this point a sick man. This is supported by the fact that his preaching in Athens lacked its normal fervour, if we are to judge by the sermon-summary in Acts 17.22-31, and that he later speaks of having reached Corinth, which he visited immediately after leaving Athens, 'feeling far from strong, . . . nervous, and rather shaky' (I Cor. 2.3 —Phillips). But there is no mention in Acts of Silvanus and Timothy rejoining Paul at Athens. They first reappear in the narrative after he had been some time in Corinth and we are told that they came from Macedonia (Acts 18.5).

LUKE'S SUMMARY

Luke, the author of the Book of Acts, has however made no attempt to record every movement of every missionary in the thirty years covered by his book. His aim is to paint the picture of the spread of the Faith in bold outline, with particular detail when he feels it to be essential to the narrative. It is not surprising therefore that he would not consider it necessary to give the prosaic account of what probably happened. Paul was in a sufficiently distressed condition when he reached Athens to send word back to Macedonia that Silvanus and Timothy should come to him at once. This they did, bringing the latest news, and Paul's concern for the church at Thessalonica, subjected to the attacks which he knew must be straining their loyalty to their new found faith, was so great that he commissioned Timothy to return to them at once. Silvanus remained with him at Athens until Paul, though still far from well, insisted that he too should return to Macedonia to look after the church at Beroea.

This is not only what we should expect from Paul, whose first concern was for his children in God, but it also squares the narrative of Acts with our epistle. The arrival of Silvanus and Timothy with the glad news of the wonderful progress of the Macedonian churches is recorded in Acts 18.5 and in v. 6 of this chapter. Luke has merely omitted the interlude of Silvanus and Timothy hastening to the side of their sick leader at Athens. Compared with the other disasters and afflictions that overtook Paul in his lifetime, Luke probably felt that this was of small moment (cf. II Cor. 11.23 ff.).

A WORTHY REPRESENTATIVE

So Timothy was sent back to Thessalonica to follow up the original apostolic mission, to bring fresh courage to the little community, and to lead them into a deeper understanding of their new faith. Paul goes out of his way to emphasize the status of his ambassador. He is not content to call him BROTHER, as he usually does elsewhere, but adds GOD'S MINISTER IN THE GOSPEL OF CHRIST. Timothy as we know was the junior member of the team, and seems to have been none too sure of himself (I Cor. 16.10-11). Paul wants to make it clear that it was no slight on the Thessalonian church to send the least impressive of the three missionaries, for Timothy like the others was a fully accredited member of Christ's Church. A variant reading is 'fellow-worker with God' (R.V. margin), a typical Pauline phrase.

It is obvious from v. 3 that the little group of Christians

E

at Thessalonica were having a difficult time. What their
AFFLICTIONS were is not stated. It was no doubt a con-
tinuation of the opposition that had driven the apostles from
the city in the first instance. Had the Jews a hand in it
too? This is at any rate a possibility. The word translated MOVED is used in two ways. It can either mean 'to
be disturbed' or 'to be beguiled'. If it is the former, then
Timothy's main task was to encourage the little church to
stand up to whatever abuse and unpopularity it received
at the hands of its pagan neighbours. If it is the latter it
would suggest that the Jews were losing no opportunity of
profiting by this to indulge in the whispering campaign
against the apostles which has already been mentioned
(2.1-12). This might well have been a more insidious threat
than direct hostility, and might be the reason for Paul's
anxiety to have Timothy on the spot as quickly as possible.

THE LAW OF THE CHRISTIAN LIFE

Paul had warned them beforehand that they must expect
opposition—from their relatives and from the pagan
priesthood. No doubt the Jews were suggesting that a faith
that aroused so much antipathy must have some serious
flaw. But the apostle seems to go further than merely saying
that in the circumstances hostility is to be expected. He
suggests that suffering is an essential part of the Christian
life. Elsewhere he speaks of the Christian believer as bear-
ing part of the sufferings of Christ (Col. 1.24), a profound
insight which takes us very near to the heart of the mystery
of pain (v. 4).

So, concludes Paul, I could no longer endure the strain
of anxiety as to how you were faring and sent Timothy to
find out whether your faith was standing up to the various
attacks which were being made upon it. Were you being
coaxed away from your staunch adherence to our Lord by
the smooth persuasiveness of his enemies? The TEMPTER

here of course is the same as Satan in 2.18—the prompter of the Jews. It was they who were determined that the apostle's missionary LABOUR SHOULD BE IN VAIN, they and their master, the Devil.

TIMOTHY'S NEWS
3.6-10

Now Paul goes on to deal with Timothy's return. By this time the apostle had reached Corinth and had established contact with two refugees from Rome. Rioting had broken out there in A.D. 49 which, according to Suetonius, originated among the Jews and was instigated by one 'Chrestus'. At this early stage in the history of the Church, the Romans made no clear distinction between Jews and Christians. While therefore it is possible that there was a Jewish revolutionary called Chrestus who was responsible for the trouble, it is generally thought that the rioting was the Jewish reaction to an attempt of unknown Christian evangelists to proclaim the gospel in the synagogues. The result was that the Emperor Claudius issued an edict expelling the Jews from Rome. Not all of them left, but among those who did were Aquila and Priscilla, who had now settled in Corinth. They were probably Christians but certainly tentmakers, and it was doubtless for both these reasons that it was in their house in Corinth that Paul lodged in the early stages of his eighteen months stay there.

While recovering his health and spirits (cf. I Cor. 2.3) he worked at his trade and conducted what seems to have been a modest type of mission on the sabbaths (Acts 18.1-4). The arrival of Silvanus and Timothy from Macedonia with the news that set Paul's mind at rest gave him fresh heart and he launched out into a preaching compaign with his normal enthusiasm (Acts 18.5). This was the point at which this letter was written, and Paul in v. 6

describes his reactions. He had been uncertain about so many things: uncertain as to whether his ordinary missionary technique would succeed in this new field with its different people and different problems: uncertain of how well his Macedonian converts would stand up to pagan opposition and Jewish innuendo: uncertain above all of himself, after his failure at Athens.

GLAD TIDINGS

But now all doubt had gone. Timothy had brought nothing but GLAD TIDINGS from Thessalonica. The little church there was as steadfast in its FAITH in the God whom Christ revealed as when the apostles had to leave it so abruptly (Acts 17.10). It was renowned far and wide for its example of Christian devotion (1.6-8). But Paul had an equally good report of the complementary element in the Christian life—their LOVE for one another. Belief and conduct were bound together in an impregnable witness to the reality of their conversion.

Further, despite all attempts to sow distrust of the apostle's motives in the minds of the Thessalonians, Paul learns that their affection for him is undiminished. They are as eager to have a visit from him as he is to pay it. The cumulative effect of all this good news on Paul is that his own troubles are forgotten. As we have seen he had had more than his share of these lately. But what he had just heard was enough to fill him with new zest and courage to tackle the vast problems that faced him in the paganism of cosmopolitan Corinth. What he had learned of the staunch FAITH of the Thessalonians was exactly the tonic that he needed.

THE JOYS OF LIVING

Verse 8 is a remarkable statement and Paul means every

word of it. Jesus himself had said (John 10.10) that he had
come into the world in order that men should know what
life meant, that they should experience in the richest and
fullest sense what we sometimes flippantly call 'the joys of
living'. The Christian gospel is just that. For most of us,
however, inside and outside the Church, the joys of living
are a poor caricature of what they might be and ought to
be. But Paul had found the secret on the Damascus road
and from then on life was lived on a plane of insight and
experience to which few since his day have attained. For
few have given their lives so utterly to their fellow men.
Life in Christ meant for Paul life for others. To give his
work, his thought, his prayers, his strength that others
should share this incomparable transformation of everything that he had ever seen or known or done or
experienced, this was what he lived for. That the little
Thessalonian church was unwavering in its obedience to
God and loyalty to Christ was for him indeed a 'breath
of life' (Phillips).

THANKS TO GOD

But, characteristically, Paul turns his thoughts to God
(v. 9). This good news is no merit of his, or of the Thessalonians for that matter. For none of it could have come
about without the grace of God. It was God who made it
possible for the little church to come into existence, just
as it was God who enabled it to STAND FAST. In giving God
the thanks they are only giving him back his own, and
not even that, for how could they give God the measure
of thanks that are his due? When Paul speaks of giving
thanks FOR YOU he does not of course mean 'on your
behalf' but 'on account of you'.

A REALISTIC PASTOR

Paul ends this passage by referring again to his fervent wish to see his Thessalonian friends again (v. 10). But in the last few words he paves the way for the topics with which he deals in the remaining two chapters of this letter, and in his second letter. Paul was a realistic pastor. He meant what he said when he thanked God for the steadfastness of faith which the Thessalonian church had exhibited, but he was not blind to the fact that their faith was far from perfect. They had the heart of the matter in them but there were many points on which they needed instruction.

The missionary campaigns of the early Church followed the familiar pattern of revivalist campaigns and faith missions in our own day. In their harvest of dedicated lives they laid the foundations of growth in character and understanding. But that is only the first step towards the establishment of the right relationship to God. Sudden conversion needs to be followed by instruction. We are not saved from ignorance, folly or superstition when we first commit our lives to Christ. We are only at the beginning of a long process of enlightenment of mind and conscience.

So despite all the words of praise which he has bestowed on the Thessalonian converts for the fervour of their faith, the constancy of their witness, and their loyalty to the apostles, Paul is under no illusion about the gaps in their knowledge of Christian doctrine or the flaws in their apprehension of the Christian ethic.

As a good pastor he has given commendation where it was deserved, but he will not hesitate to point out the shortcomings of his little flock. If he cannot do it in person he will do it by letter. But before doing so he voices a prayer.

PAUL'S PRAYER
3.11-13

Firstly Paul, knowing that God alone can bring our desires to fruition, lays before him the concern that is uppermost in his mind, that he might be permitted to revisit Thessalonica. Since he has already said that it was Satan who prevented him from returning, only one who was stronger than Satan could defeat him. If our interpretation is correct that would mean that only God could over-rule the ill-will of the Jews and circumvent their plan to keep the apostle at a safe distance from Thessalonica.

JESUS AND GOD

The English versions do not indicate what is clear in the original, namely that the word DIRECT is used in the singular although the subject is plural. The significance of this is plain. Theologically Father and Son are distinct, but for Paul God the Father and the Lord Jesus are synonymous. As a devout Jew, Paul had never worshipped any other than the one true God. When he became a Christian he worshipped Jesus Christ as Lord, and when the Church called Jesus 'Lord' they used the word which Greek-speaking Jews had always used for 'God'.

The apostle like any other early Jewish Christian would never for a moment have said that he had added a second God to the Being whom his fathers had worshipped. By the same token he would have denied that he had substituted Christ for the traditional God of Israel. What he would have said is that it was only when he came to know Jesus that he really came to know God. In worshipping Christ as Lord he was worshipping the same God as before but with an insight and understanding of his nature and purpose which had only come since he became a man in Christ.

CHRISTIAN LOVE

But even if God does not grant this request—and it was some years before Paul was able to visit Thessalonica again (Acts 20.1)—the apostle prays that the little church may be given grace to deepen their affection and intensify their care, not only for each other, but for all men, including their enemies. This prayer is so much in the spirit of Jesus (Matt. 5.46 ff.) that only God could enable them to begin to live up to it. Yet Paul could lay his hand on his heart and say in all humility that God had made it possible for him to love his Thessalonian friends with the selfless love that the gospel words demanded.

WHEN HE COMES

In the conclusion of his prayer he points back to a phrase which he has already used in describing the behaviour of the missionaries at Thessalonica (2.10) and asks that God may enable the members of the little church so to live that they will have nothing to reproach themselves with in the sight of God. Characteristically however in this letter his thought is focused on the Second Advent of Christ. The reappearance of the Messiah in Triumph, already referred to in 1.10 and in 2.19, and alluded to more fully in the next chapter (see note on 4.13) is regarded as the impending climax of history. Paul's prayer is that the Thessalonian Christians may be ready for it.

SAINTS AND ANGELS

What does Paul mean, however, by Christ coming WITH ALL HIS SAINTS? The Greek word *hagioi* which is sometimes translated SAINTS and sometimes 'holy ones' is generally in Paul's letters the word which is used for the ordinary members of the Christian Church. It cannot mean that here since it is the Thessalonian SAINTS who are to be UNBLAMEABLE IN HOLINESS when Christ comes WITH ALL HIS SAINTS. There are three common views and commentators are almost equally divided in their opinions.

(a) Paul may mean angels. He speaks in II 1.7 of the coming of the 'Lord Jesus from heaven with the angels of his power'. But he uses the normal Greek word for angels in that passage and might have been expected to use it here if that is what he meant.

(b) Paul may mean the members of the Church who have died before Christ's Second Coming. In the next chapter (4.14) he speaks of them returning with Christ then.

(c) Some commentators think he means both angels and the faithful departed.

IMAGERY AND DOCTRINE

Whichever of these views is correct the main point to note is that in this case, as in the further treatment of the Second Advent of Christ later on in this letter and in the second epistle, we should not press too closely the phraseology that the apostle uses and try to construct from it a clear-cut statement of doctrine. The whole treatment of the *Parousia*, or Second Advent of Christ, is so strongly coloured by Old Testament phraseology in these letters that it is not improbable that Paul is not hammering out Christian theology at all, as he does for example in the letter to the Romans, but echoing words which were familiar to him in connection with the Old Testament Day of the Lord, which in Jewish Christian minds strongly influenced their conception of the Second Advent. As we shall see, basically both ideas were the same, and implied the ultimate Triumph of God, the vindication of the righteous and the punishment of the wicked.

With the identification of Christ with God, which took place right from the beginning of Christian times, words and phrases from Jewish eschatology relating to the final Judgment, the coming of the Messiah, and the establishment of the Kingdom of God, would naturally be transferred to the Christian conception of the Second Advent. But they would not necessarily imply a clearly thought out Christian theology of the Last Things. They are much more the pictorial adjuncts of a basic theological conviction about the ultimate Victory of Christ which is difficult to describe in anything but liturgical language.

OLD TESTAMENT ECHOES

In this case, for example, the words Paul uses seem to be an echo of Zech. 14.5 in the Greek version, where in speaking of the great Day of the Lord the words used are: 'and the Lord my God shall come, and all the saints [or holy ones] with him'. What is referred to here is the angelic host which in the imaginative conception of later Old Testament theology contributed to the unutterable majesty of God. It is an indication of how this type of imagery was transferred from the Jewish conception of the Day of the Lord to the Jewish Christian conception of the Second Advent of Christ, that this passage from Zechariah is quoted literally in the early Christian work 'The Teaching of the Twelve Apostles' (16.7) and applied to the Second Coming of Christ with the faithful departed.

When a similar phrase is used poetically of the descent of Yahweh to give the Law to Moses on Mount Sinai ('on his right hand were his angels with him' Deut. 33.2 LXX) we should not expect it to be any less poetical when it is used of the Second Coming of the Messiah in the gospels (Mark 8.38; Matt. 25.31) or in this letter. In all cases the

phrase seems to be intended to enhance the impressiveness
of the appearance of the Divine Being.

HALF WAY MARK

At this point some of the older MSS. add *Amen*, which
may be a liturgical response. It reminds us however that
we have come to the end of the first part of the letter, which
might have been the end of the whole letter had there
been no practical problems with which Paul wanted to deal.
His theme has been wholehearted thanksgiving for the good
progress of the Church at Thessalonica and a message of
warm affection for his children in God, coupled with a
repudiation of attacks that were being made on him behind
his back and an explanation of his absence. He now turns
to deal with several matters of importance in the light of
what Timothy had told him about what was happening in
Thessalonica.

IV

SOME SPECIAL PROBLEMS
4.1-5.22

(a) PROBLEMS OF MORALS
4.1-12

Doubtless the points with which the apostle deals in the last two chapters of this letter are inspired by what he had been told by Timothy of conditions in Thessalonica and of some specific items of faith and practice on which the Christian community have asked for clarification. Yet Paul does not claim to be imparting any new teaching. What he says now is merely re-emphasizing instruction he had already given during the mission campaign. He uses the word which is technically employed elsewhere in his letters for the 'receiving' (v. 1) of missionary teaching (cf. 2.13). This was the common Christian tradition—both doctrinal and ethical—which was handed on from the original followers of Jesus and witnesses of his Resurrection to the outer ring of evangelists who carried the message far and wide throughout the Roman Empire.

Paul deliberately distinguishes between instruction which originates from himself, his own interpretation of the gospel, and the hard core of tradition which as a missionary, originally dependent on the inner circle for his knowledge of the actual words of Jesus and the events of his ministry, he had 'received' in order to hand it on in his campaigns (cf. I Cor. 15.3 with I Cor. 7.25 and I Cor. 7.10 with I Cor. 7.12). In this case he reinforces the fact that he is merely reminding the members of the Thessalonian church of

what they have already been told as the authoritative content of Christian teaching by urging them to adhere to it
in the name of THE LORD JESUS.

They have been given not only the good news of what
God has done for man in Jesus Christ but have also been
told what kind of life God expects them to live (WALK) in
return. They have already begun to accept their obligation
as followers of Jesus. What the apostle is asking is that
they should try to do even better. The word FINALLY (v. 1)
here has the meaning of 'furthermore'.

SEXUAL BEHAVIOUR
4.3-8

The first item with which Paul deals is the matter of sex
relationships. He sets the tone for what he has to say by
reminding them of the basic fact for Christians that all
conduct is not a matter of taste or inclination but is con-
ditioned by the will of God. It is his will that we should
grow into Christ-like characters. This is what Paul means
by SANCTIFICATION (v. 3). It is the progressive strengthening
of moral fibre, deepening of charity and growth of humility
which is made possible by living in the right relationship
to God and man in worship and service. One of the aspects
of this development of the right attitude to God and man
is the avoidance of sex relationships outside marriage. It
might seem surprising that after such wholehearted and
grateful praise of the Thessalonian church, Paul should
have to emphasize this matter at all. We certainly do not
get the impression from this letter that there were any
notorious violations of normal sex behaviour as there were
in the church at Corinth (I Cor. 5.1 ff.). Nor do we need
to picture Thessalonica as a city specifically noted for its
vicious practices.

THE PAGAN ATTITUDE TO SEX

The fact is that one of the most difficult hurdles that
any pagan convert had to clear was the Christian attitude
to sex. He had been brought up in a world where poly-
gamy, concubinage, homosexuality, and promiscuity were
accepted as a matter of course. The protests of the
philosophers, Stoics, Epicureans and the rest, were of little
avail against the dissolute example set by the imperial court
and their admirers. Many of the religious cults were frankly
sexual in character, with phallic rites and sacramental
fornication as part of their worship. The word 'temple'
was in many cases synonymous with 'brothel'.

Paul did not exaggerate when he painted the picture of
sex behaviour among the pagans in his letter to the Romans
(1.26 ff.). The city from which he wrote the letters to
Thessalonica was a byword even among the pagans for its
moral depravity. Thessalonica itself was the home of at
least two notable phallic cults, the Kabeiroi and the
Dionysiacs. To grow up in an atmosphere of this kind, and
then be faced with the rigid and uncompromising demand
of Christianity for complete continence outside monoga-
mous marriage, was bound to put an enormous strain on
the loyalty of normal healthy men and women who in other
respects were prepared to adhere to Christian standards.
Whatever their previous practice had been they would be
less than human if they did not find temptation too strong
for them against such a background as their pagan
neighbours provided.

THE CHRISTIAN ATTITUDE TO SEX

It is a mark of Paul's understanding of the situation that
he accepts the possibility of lapses of this character and
simply restates the Christian attitude to the matter. He had
used much harsher language when dealing with the

religious intolerance of the Jews, who were relatively irreproachable in matters of sex behaviour (2.15). Yet he shows how important he considered the danger to be by putting it in the forefront of the problems with which he deals in this second part of his letter.

There is a difference of opinion among commentators as to the meaning of VESSEL in v. 4. Some take the view that it means 'wife', others that it means 'body'. There is no strong argument philologically for interpreting the word as meaning 'wife' and there is a strong theological argument against it. Paul is emphasizing the sanctity of human personality, of which the body is a part. To describe a wife as a VESSEL is to degrade the whole conception of Christian marriage. Where she is described as the 'weaker vessel' (I Peter 3.7) it is in contrast to the husband who is alleged to be the stronger 'vessel' and not as she would be here, if VESSEL meant 'wife', as a part of her husband's household furniture. Paul is using the word in the same sense as in II Cor. 4.7.

SELF-DISCIPLINE

His aim is to raise the whole question of sex relationships on to the highest possible plane. As he says elsewhere, the body is the temple of the Holy Spirit (I Cor. 6.19) to be offered to God as a living sacrifice (Rom. 12.1). Casual sex relationships are not permissible for Christian men and women. They mean more than the momentary gratification of a biological urge, because we are not animals but potential sons and daughters of God. The first step in the matter of acquiring a proper and healthy Christian attitude to sex is to respect one's own body as much as one's own mind. It is to be held in honour and purity. We must possess our bodies otherwise they possess us. Self-control is a primary demand upon us.

LOVE AND LUST

Paul distinguishes clearly between the normal practice of sexual intercourse in marriage, which is the gift of God (Eph. 5.28 ff.) and the PASSION OF LUST (v. 5). This is the pagan attitude. By GENTILES the apostle means all pagans who disregard the light of conscience and refuse to recognize such natural perception of the difference between right and wrong as has been given to them (cf. Rom. 1.20 ff.). He does not mean GENTILES as distinct from Jews. What is often called 'love' in modern times, Paul would more correctly describe as a pagan passion of LUST. There is little to choose between the flagrant eroticism of the Roman Empire and the skilful exploitation of the sex instinct by commercial interests in our own day.

SOCIAL REPERCUSSIONS

The apostle sees clearly that it is impossible to treat the sex instinct lightly. It is one of the most powerful and mysterious factors in human life. To represent it as a private matter of self-gratification is to overlook its social repercussions. The wrong use of the sex instinct 'wrongs our brother' (v. 6). It involves treating another person as less than a person in the full Christian sense. At its worst, as in the case of buying or selling sexual experience, it is a degradation of human personality. At its best, in premarital intercourse by mutual consent, it is a caricature of what the total union of body and mind of husband and wife can be in mutual companionship and responsibility.

Sometimes the wrong inflicted on our BROTHER, which means of course any other human being, is obvious in broken homes, illegitimacy, and transmission of disease. Sometimes it is the less obvious wrong of emotional upset, perversion of habit, weakening of moral fibre, or loss of self-respect. But any misuse of the sex instinct gives rise to complications which cannot be calculated in advance. The Church need not be apologetic or half-hearted in supporting the line taken here by Paul. We are reaping a deadly harvest by disregarding it in our twentieth-century western civilization.

A THREEFOLD ARGUMENT

Paul concludes his instruction on the matter of sex by giving three reasons why Christians may not treat sexual promiscuity lightly: (1) because if we do so we shall not escape the consequences (v. 6b): (2) because when we become Christians we pledge ourselves to total commitment of our whole personality to God (v. 7): (3) because sexual purity is no man-made ruling but the will of God himself (v. 8).

FACING THE CONSEQUENCES

(1) What does Paul mean by saying that THE LORD IS AN AVENGER? We tend to side-track the idea of God's punishment of sin and talk rather of sin's inevitable consequences. But what is the difference? The phrase that Paul uses is possibly an echo of Deut. 32.35, and we have come to regard the idea of the Avenging God as a barbaric relic of Old Testament times. But insistence on the Judgment of God upon sin and evil is as strong in the New Testament as in the Old. If we believe in God it makes nonsense of life to think that we can play fast and loose with the laws he has laid down for the right government of society.

HERE AND—

Whatever may be the sexual habits of savages, or Mohammedans, or neo-pagans does not concern us. Christians are committed to accept the rule of life which

F

has been revealed by God to us through Christ. If we fall short at any point we stand under the Judgment of God, and that is no empty phrase. Paul has already referred to it twice in this letter (1.10 and 2.16). He would support the view that if we do not listen to the prophets we have to listen to Providence. We always have to pay the price for violating the revealed will of God. It may be that the price is paid in what we can see to be the direct or indirect consequences of our actions. That is the Avenging Lord.

—HEREAFTER

But there is a sense in which the Judgment that we daily bring upon ourselves must reach a climax, when the consequences of a lifetime of wasted opportunities, violation of what we know to be the laws of God and wrongs committed against our fellows must be shouldered. At that final Judgment, of which Paul has more to say later in this letter, we shall again have to do with the Avenging Lord. Like the Thessalonians we have been forewarned.

BODY AND SOUL

(2) Paul reminds his readers, and us, of the obligations that we have taken upon ourselves by committing our lives to Christ. We have been CALLED. Through no merit of our own God has laid his hand upon us and has given us grace to respond. Our allegiance is thenceforth to him and the way of life he has revealed to us. That way involves the day to day battle with temptation. It means falling and rising again, repentance and renewal. But as a basis it implies our dedication of body and mind to God's service. There is no room in the Christian life for UNCLEANNESS, whether we dignify it by high-sounding psychological terminology such as the need for sexual self-expression, or, like Paul, call a spade a spade and describe it as LUST.

THE TEMPLE OF THE HOLY SPIRIT

(3) The apostle has put forward as reasons for a distinctive Christian attitude to sex behaviour, firstly, a wholesome fear of the consequences of the wrong use of the sex instinct, secondly, the fact that we are committed to a way of life which has no place in it for sexual promiscuity. He now adduces the third and highest ground, that to treat our bodies and other people's bodies as a means of providing erotic pleasure outside the complete man-woman relationship of marriage is not only an offence against society but against the Creator and his image in which each one of us is made.

Our bodies are holy because God has put his Spirit within us. We are more than a combination of nerve cells and biological urges. We are Christs in the making. To regard ourselves or others as anything less is not only to destroy the right relationship between two personalities but also between our own personality and God. It is the presence of his Spirit within us that raises us above the rest of the created world, that differentiates us from the instinctive level of animal behaviour. When we behave as if there were no such differentiation we cease to have the right to call ourselves men and women. Each time we treat our body or someone else's body as less than a Temple of the Holy Spirit we push ourselves and them that much further down the ladder that connects us with God and break that relationship which is the only way to the fulfilment of our personalities.

BROTHERLY LOVE
4.9-12

The next few verses deal with some general principles which are admirably suited to the life of any Christian

community at any time. The items Paul mentions may
occur in this letter because of some particular information
given by Timothy, or they may simply be good pastoral
advice from a wise father in God who wanted to ensure
that his little flock was in every way a credit to the Lord
Jesus Christ.

Their record of brotherly love was outstanding. Paul
means no vague feelings of goodwill towards one another
but mutual help and hospitality. When he reflected on this
new-found consideration and concern he could not but
recognize that only God had instilled it into them. Nor
was their care for each other confined to their own little
circle, they were ready to help the whole Christian community in Macedonia.

Although we only know of Christian churches in Philippi,
Thessalonica and Beroea, there must have been many more
Christian families and individuals whose business took
them to other parts of the country. As the capital city and
a busy seaport Thessalonica would naturally have more
than its share of visitors, to whom the local churchpeople
opened their homes and their hearts. Paul urges them to
continue this good work.

SECOND ADVENTISM

He then mentions three items which are equally evidence
of 'brotherly love'. STUDY TO BE QUIET: DO YOUR OWN
BUSINESS: WORK WITH YOUR HANDS. In view of the more
detailed reference in II 3.6 ff. to a certain element of rest-
lessness among a section of the Christian community at
Thessalonica these words are probably best understood as
a mild caution prompted by what Timothy had reported.
It appears that as a result of excited anticipation of the
impending end of the world—with which the apostle deals
next—there was an unsettled atmosphere in the community.

We may imagine a situation such as attends some

religious revivals where an unhealthy emotionalism pre-
vails and where people need to be reminded that it is a
primary duty of a Christian to get on with his job and
behave like an ordinary sensible citizen. There is a reference
in II 3.11 to 'busybodies' which suggests that this injunction to the members of the Thessalonian church to 'mind
their own business' is directed to the few hot-heads who
were rushing about excitedly speculating about the crack
of doom.

NO ROOM FOR PARASITES

In the same passage in his second letter the apostle has
to speak more plainly about those who have knocked off
work on a plea of the imminent end of the world and are
quite content to sponge off their neighbours in the meantime. Apparently the situation by that time had become
more acute—hence part of the reason for a second letter—
but we may take these remarks of Paul here as being
directed to an early stage of Second Advent hysteria on
the part of a few of the Thessalonians.

Paul had not only CHARGED them to work with their
hands, he had set them a good example (cf. 2.9). The normal
Greek attitude to manual labour was that it was good
enough for slaves but not for self-respecting citizens.
Probably the majority of the Thessalonian church consisted of slaves who were normally artisans, and Paul is
here emphasizing the dignity of labour as a Christian virtue.
In this attitude Christianity was true to its Jewish heritage.
It was important both for the good name of the community
and for the good of their own souls that every one of them
should be independent and self-supporting. There is no
room for parasites in the Christian community.

PAUL'S ADVICE TO CHRISTIANS

1. *Keep your head*

While we may see in this threefold counsel a needed admonition to people in the grip of religious emotionalism, tense with expectancy of the approaching End, it may well be taken as a guide to Christians at any time and in any place. A Christian ought to be an oasis of tranquillity in this hectic, bustling world with all its perplexities and tensions. He is anchored to the one reality in the universe: he is in touch with the one source of stability. He is not immune from the anxieties and pressures of modern life but he knows where to turn for strength to face them.

2. *Mind your own business*

Similarly it is always a temptation to confuse Christian service with interfering in other people's business. There is a difference between a proper concern for our neighbour's needs and a relentless determination to save his soul or reform his character. We are not called upon to take upon our own shoulders all the problems and difficulties that afflict the world or even our own circle of friends. Tact and sympathy, which are also Christian virtues, must come to our aid and warn us to 'mind our own business' when we are carried away by our good intentions.

3. *Pull your weight*

As for the Christian attitude to hard work, it is still as true with a forty-hour week as it was in Paul's day, when the working hours were more than twice as long, that the virtue does not reside in the hardness of the work but in the conscientiousness with which we do what we are paid to do. Paul would not have said that there was any more virtue from a Christian point of view in the 'hardness' of a navvy's job than in that of a draper or a student. To work with the brain or the hands is not the point at issue.

But to give of one's best, whatever the job may be, is where work becomes worship and part of our offering to God.

(b) PROBLEMS OF BELIEF
4.13–5.11

NOTE ON THE SECOND ADVENT OF CHRIST

Having dealt with some matters of behaviour which were causing trouble or were liable to cause trouble within the Thessalonian community, Paul proceeds to some problems of belief. The fact that the two specific items with which he deals are both connected with the Second Coming of Christ, and that his second letter to Thessalonica is largely concerned with the same question gives the Thessalonian correspondence a characteristically eschatological flavour.

IN THE KERYGMA

It is sometimes suggested that the original gospel preached by the apostles at Thessalonica during the mission must have given this specific doctrine particular emphasis. There is no reason to suppose that this was so. The early stages of the missionary preaching of the Church included as one of its elements the proclamation of the imminent return of our Lord. The Scriptures had been fulfilled, Messiah had come. Through the evil designs of men he had been done to death, but God had overruled their crime and revealed Jesus of Nazareth in his true light by raising him from the dead. He had been exalted to God's right hand as Lord of all. But God in his mercy offered men a last chance to repent of their sins, for soon Messiah would return to judge the world. Evil would be destroyed and

those who had by baptism been incorporated into the
Christian fellowship would be saved.

AT THESSALONICA

This was the gospel preached at Thessalonica as elsewhere. The only reason why Paul devotes so great a part
of his letters to the Thessalonians to dealing with aspects
of one particular element in this common proclamation is
that he had learned, either from Timothy or elsewhere,
that there was a need for clearer instruction on this topic
and that certain misunderstandings had to be removed.

IN THE THOUGHT OF PAUL

It is also suggested that the detailed account of the
Return of Christ given in these letters forms an early stage
of the apostle's thought and that he later departed from it.
There is no evidence for this view either. On the contrary
it is clear from references in Paul's later letters that his
expectation of the speedy return of Christ was maintained
to the end (cf. Col. 1.22; Phil. 1.10; 4.5). In this he shared
the view of the early Church as a whole. The only change
that took place in Paul's thinking on this matter was that
as he faced the prospect of death he doubted whether he
himself would live to see the *Parousia* (see note on 4.15).

A FUNDAMENTAL BELIEF

This ought to lead us to consider what was in fact the
essential nature of the belief of the early Church in the
Second Advent. Why did it form such a constant element
in missionary propaganda, and why, when it did not take
place as soon as it had been expected, did the Church not
consider that the gospel proclamation had been fundamen-
tally wrong? It was obviously not regarded as a side issue.
The repeated references to it in this letter already (1.10;

2.19; 3.13) indicate that it was of the highest importance. Indeed we must be grateful that it did become such an urgent matter for the apostle to settle these minor problems at Thessalonica since it lets us see how important an element the Second Advent was in the early Church.

OLD TESTAMENT THOUGHT-FORMS

We must however distinguish between the substance of the belief in the Second Advent and the form in which it was expressed. We are assisted in this by a growing recognition of how much the thought of the early Church was affected by the Old Testament and in how many ways this can be observed. Old Testament theology was not speculative but practical. Its writers had certain basic convictions which had been revealed to them. But when they came to express them they normally used the language of myth and symbol. They knew nothing of our western scientific literalism but worked rather with images, poetic figures, and pictorial illustrations. They expressed the truths they wished to convey by suggestion rather than by factual statement and they were robustly anthropomorphic in that they had no hesitation in describing divine activity in terms of human experience. The stories of Adam and Eve, Noah and Jonah are good examples of their methods.

They further recognized certain recurring patterns of God's activity in dealing with man: Creation and Fall, Death and Resurrection, Judgment and Mercy, Humiliation and Triumph. Some of these patterns they saw working out in history, in the life of their own people and of the world in general. Others they held as basic convictions consequent on their fundamental belief about God.

THE BEGINNING

Because the Bible is a unity, and the writers of the New

Testament were largely Jews, we must expect to find the
same modes of expressing theological truth and the same
patterns of belief in the New Testament as in the Old.
When therefore we encounter in the Thessalonian letters
or in the Book of Revelation a highly coloured description
of what will happen at the end of the world, we must not
regard it as in any sense a more factual description than
is the account of the origin of the world in the Book of
Genesis. In both cases the language is that of the poet
and not of the scientist. The Hebrews had no more information about the origins of the universe than had the
Babylonians or the Egyptians. But as distinct from the
Babylonians who believed that it started with a battle
between the sun-god and a dragon-goddess, and the
Egyptians who attributed it to an act of self-abuse on
the part of the creator, they maintained as a postulate of
faith that it was the rational expression of the mind and
will of the one Supreme Being who is Lord of all life and
history.

THE END

Similarly they had no revealed information about how
the world would end. But they had, again as a postulate
of faith, the conviction that it would end sometime and
that it would finally be restored to what had been in the
mind of God before man's sin and folly had made a caricature of it. It was their unshakable belief in the nature and
purpose of the God who had been revealed to them that
led the religious leaders of Israel to the conviction that the
end of the time-process must be the visible victory of God
over all the forces of evil. They were well aware that it
was only a tiny handful within a totally insignificant
political unit that shared this conviction. But so stubbornly
did they hold it that, despite all appearances and indications to the contrary, they never wavered in their belief

that one day God would prove to the world that their faith was true.

THE DAY OF YAHWEH

The earliest form of this belief was highly nationalistic in character. One day the Gentiles would learn that Israel was Yahweh's chosen people. Their oppression of his elect nation would be punished and Israel would lord it over his enemies. This was to be the great Day of the Lord. But even with this strongly self-centred flavour it should be noted that the emphasis was on Yahweh and not on Israel. The prophets had made short work of this arrogant interpretation of history. They proclaimed that the Day of the Lord would indeed come but it would be a day when God would vindicate righteousness and punish evil wherever it was found, and Israel would be judged like the rest. The prophets did not explain how this would happen. They did however maintain that it would take place in the world that men knew and that it was liable to happen at any moment (e.g. Amos 5.20 ff.).

PROPHETIC HOPE

Following the Day of the Lord would come the Golden Age of peace, mercy and righteousness when all hatred and oppression would be no more (e.g. Isa. 2.2-4). But the prophets provided no programme of events and no timetable. Their basic contention was founded on their insight into the nature of a God who would not allow evil to triumph for ever. It followed from that that the more strongly they believed in his righteousness the nearer they believed the destruction of evil to be. Thus the time factor was incidental. It was a matter of faith and not of the calendar.

FORLORN HOPE

After the days of the prophets two modifications of this belief set in. As Israel found itself reduced to political and economic insignificance after the Exile, and as one great power after another stepped on to the stage of history and dominated the world by force of arms and ruthless methods, the Golden Age seemed to many a pious dream. Here was a nation living in accordance with God's revealed will, a theocratic community, governed by God's priests and administered by his Law, yet still evil flourished and the oppressors and idolators of the world lorded it over the people of God.

A NEW FORM OF AN OLD HOPE

But the religious leaders of Israel never lost their faith in his providence. They claimed that the prophets had not been wrong. They had only underestimated the power of evil in the world at large. So corrupt had the world become that it was beyond redemption. The Golden Age would come, but not in the world that men knew. This old evil world would disappear at the bidding of God: a new heaven and a new earth would take its place, and the blessed life of the Age to Come would be shared by God's faithful servants while his enemies would meet the fate they deserved (cf. Joel 2.28-32).

MESSIAH

The second modification of the prophetic eschatology was the result of the growing emphasis on the remoteness and otherness of God. While the prophets had thought of the Golden Age as being inaugurated by God or some human representative, it was in keeping with the development of supernatural ideas that in the period between the

Old Testament and the New Testament the Golden Age should be conceived of as inaugurated by a supernatural figure. The Messiah, a divine deliverer sent by God, would appear with dramatic suddenness, a Judgment would take place in which the righteous would be separated from the wicked, and the Golden Age or Kingdom of God would begin in which the just would reap the fruits of their labours in the presence of God.

THE KINGDOM OF GOD IS AT HAND

There were of course innumerable facets of this belief and many variations in detail. There was likewise side by side with it a persistent expectation on the part of many of a political Deliverer of the kind that the prophets had fore-told, but that this hope of the advent of a supernatural Messiah was strongly held by many Jews at the time when Jesus began his ministry is beyond question. John the Baptist was one of them (cf. Matt. 3.1-12).

THE KINGDOM OF GOD HAS COME

His message was of the imminent appearance of Messiah in fire and judgment, and of the impending end of this wicked world. Jesus, although he avoided the title of Messiah, since it had for so many people a political impli-cation, made it plain by all that he did and said that he regarded his rôle as that of God's appointed Deliverer to save men from the power of sin and self and to inaugurate the Golden Age of the prophets' hopes, the sovereign rule of God over the world and the defeat of evil in all its forms, including disease and death. He made it equally plain, however, that his conception of Messiah was that which Deutero-Isaiah had glimpsed, the Servant of God who through his own suffering would bring men into the right relationship with God (Mark 8.27-9.1).

The Kingdom would come 'with power' through his vicarious self-offering.

THE DAY OF THE SON OF MAN

Jesus' view of his own rôle however did not end with the pain and humiliation of the Cross. He called himself Son of Man, and in so doing he clearly looked back to the vision of Daniel 7.13 of one who would reign over a new type of commonwealth, the society of those who had committed their lives to God. Jesus looked beyond the ignominy of the Cross to a future Triumph. His instructions to his disciples, however, were to go out into all the world and preach the gospel. The implication of that is that the final Judgment and God's victory over evil would not take place until all men had been given the opportunity to repent and turn to God (Matt. 24.14; Mark 13.10).

ON EARTH OR IN HEAVEN?

But much of the language that Jesus used appeared to suggest that he envisaged his imminent return to earth. Careful examination of his words however indicates that in some cases at least what looks like a prophecy of his return is in fact a prophecy of his Resurrection and Ascension (e.g. Mark 14.61-62). We must admit that it is impossible on the gospel evidence to say whether our Lord did envisage his future Triumph as taking place on this earth as he knew it or in the vastly different sphere of the full realization of the Age to Come. What we can say, however, in view of his obvious intention to found the Church, and his marching orders to the disciples, is that he did not think in terms of a speedy end to their mission.

JESUS OF NAZARETH IS THE MESSIAH

But when the first missionaries set out on their task it

was inevitable that the imminent return of the Messiah should become a feature of their message. They were Jews who had searched the scriptures. There they had found in Deutero-Isaiah confirmation of Jesus' puzzling references to his sufferings and death (cf. Isa. 53). They were convinced that he was Messiah: here then was the explanation of why Messiah had been crucified, a fact which according to the Law put him into the category of a felon accursed of God, to say nothing of exploding his claim to be Messiah.

THE MESSIANIC SIGNS

They were likewise convinced by the Resurrection, following the miracles during his ministry, further authenticated by Pentecost, the gift of ' tongues ', ecstatic prophecy and other manifestations of the supernatural, that the Last Days foretold by the prophets had dawned; the Age to Come had begun (e.g. Acts 2.14 ff.). But only a few acknowledged this. The world went on its way unheeding. Evil continued unchecked. Surely there must be some visible indication given by God to the world at large that Jesus of Nazareth was indeed Messiah, that his mastery over sin and death was an earnest of their final annihilation. God's righteousness must be seen to be vindicated.

JESUS CHRIST IS LORD

What then would be more natural than that they should, as it were, write the last chapter before the story was finished and round off the plan of salvation with an affirmation of this ultimate vindication of God and his Messiah as the final element in the gospel message, and what more natural than that they should do so in the language of the Old Testament passages where God's supremacy is asserted? The Church had from the beginning worshipped

Jesus as Lord, giving him the title which the Greek-speaking Jews had used of God. What the Old Testament had said about God the New Testament can say about Jesus, since Jesus is for the early Church the express image of his person (Heb. 1.3).

THE DAY OF CHRIST

Accordingly when the early missionaries wished to express their conviction of the final victory of Christ and his gospel over the evil that still abounded they did so in echoes of the language which Old Testament prophecy had used of the final victory of God. The Day of the Lord became the Day of Christ (Phil. 1.10). In these Thessalonian letters, which we may take together with the Book of Acts as reflecting the earliest stratum of missionary preaching, we shall not have to look far beyond the Old Testament for the imagery and symbolism which are used in the description of the Second Advent of Christ.

CHRISTIAN HOPE AND JEWISH APOCALYPTIC

Paul is not giving us a programme of the end events of time and history, in the manner of the Jewish apocalyptic writings of the inter-testamental period. He is sharing with us the theological conviction of the early Church that the end of everything will be the Triumph of Christ, when every knee shall bow of things in heaven and things on earth, and every tongue confess that he is Lord (Phil. 2.10-11). We are therefore ill-advised to take these passages in any more literal manner than we should take similar passages in the Old Testament where the majesty and glory of God are described in the imaginative language of poetic symbol, which is the only language in which men can describe mysteries they can do no more than hint at.

IMMINENCE NOT IMMEDIACY

It is a further misunderstanding of the nature of early Church theology to lay stress on the fact that the Second Advent of Christ was expected to take place within the lifetime of the first Christians. The prophets had used similar language of the Day of the Lord. It was always just at hand, as is the Return of Christ in the New Testament. But this is nothing more than the expression of the intensity of their conviction. Heaven had come to earth. They were living already in the Age to Come. The rapid spread of the gospel, the miraculous conversion of the Gentiles (and where more miraculous than in the heart of pagan cities like Thessalonica and Corinth?), the powerful presence of the Spirit in their midst, all tended to intensify the sense of an impending consummation of their hopes.

BETWEEN THE TIMES

It is significant that when the end did not come as they expected no vital sense of loss was experienced. The Church adjusted itself to the realization that the Triumph of Christ was something that lay far ahead and that it had many battles to fight and much tribulation to endure before the final event in history should bring to an end the interregnum between the First and Second Advents of their Lord. We ourselves still live in the period between the times, between the heralding of the Kingdom of God in Christ's incarnation and its final consummation in his Triumph. Our life is lived at the same time in this age and in the age to come (I Cor. 10.11).

CHRISTUS VICTOR

We shall do well as we follow the apostle's thought in this passage if we regard his words not as literal prophecy,

G

nor yet as outmoded Jewish apocalyptic, still less as a
dream that did not come true, but as the basic conviction
of the ultimate Victory of Christ which all Christians must
share, couched in the only kind of language in which such
a conviction can be expressed.

THE DEAD WILL SHARE IN
CHRIST'S TRIUMPH
4.13-18

It is against this general background of missionary
preaching of the *Parousia* as part of the gospel that Paul
proceeds to deal with the two specific aspects of it referred
to in 4.13-18 and 5.1-11. The first section deals with a
problem which presumably had been put to Timothy by
the Thessalonians, and which had apparently not previously
been dealt with during the mission.

THE THESSALONIANS' PROBLEM

The missionaries had left the little group of converts in
Thessalonica exhilarated by their new-found faith, caught
up in an experience of a new quality of life, liberated from
the frustrations of paganism, with their whole existence
focused on Christ as Saviour and Lord. Responding to the
urgent challenge of the apostles they found themselves
living in a new dimension. In Biblical language they lived
already in the Age to Come, and felt, as always in times
of intense spiritual awareness, that its visible consummation was at hand. The final triumph of the gospel and the
victory of Christ over the powers of evil in which they were
to share could not be far off. But a new factor had arisen
which threatened to shake their faith. Some of the converts had died before the *Parousia* took place. Did that
mean that they would not share in Christ's Triumph, had

they died too soon to take their place with their fellow members of the Thessalonian church in the blessed society of the redeemed when Christ would present his people to God at the Great Day?

THE MAKING OF CHRISTIAN THEOLOGY

This was their first question, which the apostle answers in 4.13-18 with the assurance that their loved ones are safe in God's hands and that they will suffer in no way from having died before the *Parousia*. In so far as there was as yet no provision in the earliest form of the gospel message for an intermediate state between death and the end-event of history, Paul has to make one of his many contributions to the substance of Christian theology. It may well be that he had considered the matter before, since there had already been deaths in the Christian community (Acts 12.2), but this is the first written evidence of it in his letters.

THE SLEEP OF DEATH

When he refers to the dead as those who FALL ASLEEP (v. 13) Paul is not using the words in any specifically Christian sense. Jews and pagans alike referred to death as sleep, although with its sequel in an awakening, the word is peculiarly suited to the Christian view of death as a prelude to resurrection. For Christians death holds no terrors. We should not therefore SORROW for the dead, though we shall naturally grieve over our own loss.

MEN WITHOUT HOPE

Let us rather sorrow for those who die without any Christian hope at all. In Paul's day there were various types of hope beyond death—the hope of the Jewish Pharisee in a resurrection of the body, of the Platonist in the immortality of the soul, of the devotees of the mystery cults in personal survival. Doubtless the apostle, in describing all non-Christians as having NO HOPE, is thinking of the vast masses of humanity in cities like Thessalonica to whom these esoteric beliefs meant nothing, and who shared the fatalism which is reflected on pagan tombstones. For them death meant the end of everything. Paul would say that we ought to sorrow for them—and for our neo-pagans to-day—but he might well have included all those whose hope was not founded on the present knowledge of being IN CHRIST. Only they could face death with equanimity (cf. 5.10).

OUR ANCHOR IN HISTORY

Paul now gives in v. 14 the historical foundation on which Christian hope is built. Other religions and philosophies may speculate on what may happen after death and may believe that it will happen. Only the Christian can say that his hope is founded on something that did happen. JESUS DIED AND ROSE AGAIN. Here is our anchor in history. If Christ did not rise again, as Paul says elsewhere (I Cor. 15.14) our preaching and our faith have no meaning. Nor has our Christian hope any justification if the Resurrection of Jesus did not take place.

DEATH AND RESURRECTION

Every Christian reproduces in his own life the pattern of the Death and Resurrection of Jesus. By accepting Christ as Saviour and Lord he dies to his past life and rises to new life in Christ. This is his true death and resurrection. From then on he is a man in Christ, and he remains a man in Christ despite the physical decay and death of his body. To experience physical death is then nothing other than to have FALLEN ASLEEP IN JESUS.

SHARING IN THE LORD'S TRIUMPH

This is what the Thessalonians had been taught and what they believed. What they were concerned about was the sequel and Paul now gives them the assurance. God will bring back to life those who have fallen asleep in Jesus when he brings back his Son to judge the world and consummate his kingdom. They will not be forgotten. They will be awakened from their sleep to take part in their Lord's Triumph.

The R.V. margin notes an alternative translation which is preferred by some versions and commentators: 'them also that are fallen asleep will God through Jesus bring with him'. This would mean that God would bring back the faithful dead with Jesus at his Coming through the agency or by means of Jesus. Either translation is possible from the Greek text. Parallel ideas can be found for both in other Pauline letters ((*a*) I Cor. 15.18; (*b*) I Cor. 6.14), but the R.V. translation seems to embody a more profound conception.

THE WORD OF THE LORD

Having given the assurance that the Thessalonians need have no anxiety about the fate of their loved ones, Paul proceeds to give more detailed confirmation, based on THE WORD OF THE LORD. It is not clear what he means by that. Does he mean a special revelation to himself (as in Gal. 1.12) or to Silvanus, who was also presumably an ecstatic, subject to visions like the Old Testament prophets (Acts 15.32)? Or is he referring to some saying of Jesus? If so it is not in the gospels, and if we include vv. 15-17a as the total content of the 'word', which seems to be what

Paul intended, it is quite unlike any of the *Parousia* passages which are recorded there.

THE TRADITION

On the other hand Paul speaks elsewhere of the common substance of missionary preaching and teaching as being tradition received 'from the Lord' (I Cor. 11.23). Jesus as Lord was the fulfilment of Old Testament Law and Prophecy. The gospel which the missionaries proclaimed and the instruction which they gave, based on the words and works of Jesus, illumined by the Old Testament, was in Paul's view no human tradition but was transmitted by the exalted Lord. Behind it was the guidance of the Spirit. These verses 15-17a which suggest the inexpressible final Revelation of Christ by a series of Old Testament images, originally applied to the Revelation of God, are as naturally described as THE WORD OF THE LORD as their Old Testament prototypes were described as 'the word of God'.

PAUL'S PART IN THE PAROUSIA

When Paul says WE THAT ARE ALIVE THAT ARE LEFT UNTO THE COMING OF THE LORD he obviously expects to be present at the *Parousia* himself. He shared the universal expectation that Christ's coming was not far off. Five years later when writing to the Corinthian church (A.D. 55) he still expected to live to see it (I Cor. 15.51), but his serious illness referred to in II Cor. 1.8, 9, when his life was despaired of, appears to have changed his views and when he wrote his letter to the church at Philippi he had given up hope of being still alive when the Lord came (Phil. 1.20 ff.).

THE PAROUSIA

THE COMING OF THE LORD has already been referred to

in 2.19 and 3.13. *Parousia*, the Greek word translated
COMING, originally meant 'presence' and Paul occasionally
uses it in this sense (Phil. 1.26), but generally in the New
Testament it is the word used to refer to the Second
Coming of Christ. In the everyday language of the pagan
world it was the word used for the visit of an important
official or a royal personage or the manifestation of a god.
This was the sense in which it was applied to the Second
Coming of Jesus and Paul may have been the first to use
it in this connection. It is important to remember its
original meaning, however, since the idea of Christ's
'presence' with his people from the Resurrection onwards
is not essentially different from his 'presence' with them
at his COMING. It is then that his 'presence' with his people
will be fully revealed. Similarly, it is when his people feel
his 'presence' with them most strongly—as in the early
Church—that they hope for the speedy revelation of the
fulness of his glory.

REASSURANCE

Paul goes on in v. 15 to reassure the relatives and friends
of those members of the Thessalonian community who
have already died that those who are still alive at the great
Day will not have an unfair advantage. The view that there
was a peculiar blessing attached to survival until the end-
event was expressed in Dan. 12.12. Was this possibly
another subtle thrust by the local Jews to shake the
allegiance of the converts? If so, Paul's statement is wide
enough to include not only those who have already died
but any who shall have FALLEN ASLEEP before the *Parousia*.

COMFORT NOT ESCHATOLOGY

It is obvious from what follows that Paul has no intention of giving a literal description of the end of the world.

His main concern is to comfort the sorrowing relatives of
the deceased church members. This he does in the last
clauses of vv. 16 and 17. The details of the *Parousia* are
merely a framework, part of which at least would be
known to his readers, and all of which was the traditional
picture which Paul had doubtless himself received as a
missionary, but which was built up of imagery familiar to
any Jew.

A PAINTING IN WORDS

It is a picture of a spectacular descent of Christ from
heaven, heralded by supernatural intimations, at which
point the dead are raised and the living are caught up and
both together meet the Lord in the air. Its kinship is with
a Renaissance canvas, not with a text book of theology.
Nothing is said of a Judgment, of the fate of non-Christians,
of the nature of the Resurrection-body, or of the ultimate
destination, whether heaven or a transformed earth.

OLD TESTAMENT IMAGES

The symbolism of the Ascension (Acts 1.9) is repeated
in reverse order. The Lord descends from heaven from his
session at the right hand of God (Col. 3.1) just as the
prophet Micah had pictured the descent of Yahweh from
heaven in Judgment (Micah 1.3). There is a mighty sound,
as of a trumpet, and the divine voice is heard, as when
Yahweh came down to earth at Sinai (Ex. 19.16 ff.) or as
the prophet Joel foretold of the Day of Yahweh (Joel 2.1).
The Archangel, presumably Michael (Dan. 10.13), leader
of the accompanying retinue of angels, as in Zech. 14.5
(cf. 3.13), traditionally sounds the trumpet that announces
Yahweh's approach to judge the world.

It is beside the point to enquire whether these were three
different sounds or the same sound, or to try to identify

the various elements of this picture in Jewish apocalyptic literature. The intention is obviously to convey in traditional imagery the awe-inspiring final event of history when the unutterable glory of the holiness of God as revealed in Christ is fully disclosed to the whole creation.

UNANSWERED QUESTIONS

In Paul's picture the faithful Christians who have already died are raised from their graves, and joining the faithful Christians who are still alive at the time they are CAUGHT UP IN THE CLOUDS TO MEET THE LORD IN THE AIR. Here too the details are incidental and impressionistic. Nothing is said of what has happened to the dead in the meantime. There is no suggestion of purgatory. Nor is there any mention of the transformation of the bodies of the living or of the provision of bodies for the dead to fit them for their new type of existence. The apostle makes his own contribution to Christian theology on this subject later in I Cor. 15.

THE RAPTURE

But here he merely echoes the traditional imagery of Daniel 12.2 ('many of them that sleep in the dust of the earth shall awake, some to everlasting life'). In Daniel's vision of the Last Day those whose names are 'written in the book', and are therefore still alive, will be 'delivered', and, as in Paul's view, 'some' of the dead will be raised to join them. A similar picture is to be found in Isaiah (26.19a; 21.13a, 12b). They are borne heavenwards like Elijah (II Kings 2.11) not however in chariots of fire but on the clouds that suggest the mysterious shroud that conceals divine glory from mortal men (Dan. 7.13; Acts 1.9). Then, in the space between earth and heaven, they welcome the royal visitor like the Wedding Guests

who go out to meet the Bridegroom in Matthew's parable
of the *Parousia* (Matt. 25).

AN UNFINISHED PICTURE

Again Paul paints with a broad brush. What happens
next? Do the saints join the angelic throng and return to
earth with their Lord to be present at the Judgment of
the rest of the world? Or do they proceed heavenwards?
The former would be the more natural sequel if Paul were
indeed giving us a theology of the Last Things. But clearly
his interest lies elsewhere. The nub of his argument, and
of this whole passage is the last clause of v. 17 which
should be taken together with the last clause of v. 16.
This is his real contribution.

FOR EVER WITH THE LORD

Paul's fundamental conviction emerges from this ' mosaic
of reminiscences of the prophets' that once a man is IN
CHRIST he remains IN CHRIST for ever. The Christian who
dies before the End remains in death as much IN CHRIST
as the Christian who is still alive when the time-process
comes to a stop. Beyond this age that we know and the
world that we know lies a life that can only be hinted at
and glimpsed by poet and painter. But for the Christian it
means life for EVER WITH THE LORD, and it includes the
DEAD IN CHRIST, which was what the Thessalonians wanted
to know for their COMFORT.

NEITHER DEATH, NOR LIFE . . .

The apostle had no more knowledge than the Thessalonians or ourselves of the process by which this age will
come to an end and the age to come will take its place.
The mystery that surrounds what lies beyond the death of
the body as also the ultimate Triumph of Christ and the

communion of saints in the Kingdom of God can either be a field of unprofitable speculation or, under the guidance of Paul, something that, however we conceive of it with our imaginations, remains for us a vital postulate of faith based on our knowledge of God as he has revealed himself to us in Jesus Christ (cf. Rom. 8.38-39).

WATCH AND PRAY
5.1-11

Paul now turns to the second problem of belief which is, like the first, connected with the Second Advent. His handling of it suggests that the introduction of this topic was occasioned by reports of the beginnings of irresponsible behaviour among some members of the Thessalonian community on the plea that the end of the world was at hand. The apostle has already hinted at flaws in the otherwise unblemished record of the converts (3.10) and makes reference twice in this letter to an apparent tendency on the part of some to down tools and panic (4.11; 5.14).

Paul refuses to be drawn into a discussion of when the *Parousia* will take place. He contents himself with reminding them of what they well knew, that the End when it came would be sudden and unexpected. No man could prophesy the day or the hour (Mark 13.32). But come it would, bringing disaster on those who flouted the Laws of God. Christian men, however, had nothing to fear. Nor need they interrupt their normal life to prepare for it. Their whole aim should be so to live that they are ready at any moment to meet their Judge and Maker.

TIMES AND SEASONS

The apostle begins by reminding his readers that they are already well aware of the answer to the question which was in their minds: When will the *Parousia* take place?

THE TIMES AND THE SEASONS (v. 1) is a phrase used elsewhere in the Bible and it was presumably quite common
in this connection (Dan. 2.21; Acts 1.7). Technically the
word for TIMES means duration of time, and the word for
SEASONS means decisive moments within time. The phrase
would therefore assume the question not only as to when
the Second Advent might be expected but also as to what
events might happen before it, through which Christians
would recognize that God was speaking to them.

LIKE A THIEF IN THE NIGHT

Missionary teaching, following our Lord's own words
(Luke 12.39; Matt. 24.43) had constantly emphasized that
God's final Judgment, the vindication of his righteousness
and the annihilation of evil in all its forms, would come
as suddenly and unexpectedly as a THIEF IN THE NIGHT
(v. 2). The picture is of the householder, trusting in the
security of his lockfast house, surprised and overpowered
by the violence of the intruder (John 10.10). THE DAY OF
THE LORD = the Day of the Son of Man (Luke 17.30) = the
the Day of Christ (Phil. 2.16) is the common Old Testament
usage for the ultimate revelation of the power and moral
holiness of God followed by the reward of the just and the
punishment of the wicked. Paul uses it here, of course,
with reference to the *Parousia* of the Christians' Lord (see
note on the Second Advent, p. 92).

SUDDEN DESTRUCTION

Those who ought to be concerned about the *Parousia*,
continues the apostle (v. 3), are those who have cause to
fear God's righteous Judgment. Just when they are com-
forting themselves that they can safely snap their fingers
at God and man, the cataclysm overtakes them. As
suddenly as premature labour pains seize A WOMAN WITH

CHILD inescapable retribution is upon them. In this dramatic picture of the Crack of Doom Paul echoes in milder form a common Old Testament motif (cf. Isa. 13.6-8; Ezek. 30.3 ff.; Joel 2.1 ff.; Zech. 14). It would seem, however, that once more (cf. 4.16, 17) Paul's Christian convictions shine through the conventional imagery. The word he uses for DESTRUCTION here is the same as that which he uses again in II 1.9, where it plainly means something other than physical annihilation. In both cases DESTRUCTION for Paul means final separation from Christ. This is in his view the ultimate penalty for persistent sin, and in his eyes there could be no worse punishment.

DARKNESS AND LIGHT

Then turning from the terrible fate of the evildoers at the Judgment, Paul contrasts it (vv. 4-5) with the happy prospect that faces the Christian believer. What terrors does Doomsday hold for him? Why should any Christian man be afraid to meet his Maker? If this excitement among a few of the church members at Thessalonica was the result of anxious foreboding let them take heart. Christians live in LIGHT not in DARKNESS—and here Paul plays on the connection between LIGHT and THE DAY (of the Lord) contrasted with DARKNESS and the NIGHT (of SUDDEN DESTRUCTION)—therefore the light of THE DAY OF THE LORD will not take them unawares as it will the wicked THIEF who works in the DARKNESS of NIGHT.

THE LIGHT OF THE WORLD

This emphasis on the LIGHT in which Christians live is in direct opposition to what Paul in his pre-Christian days had been taught. For the rabbis of Judaism this present age was the darkness of night. Light was the condition of the age to come. But for Paul, the Christian, the age to come had already dawned and the believer lived in the light which Christ had brought into the world. The ignorance and moral depravity of paganism were still gross darkness, but those who had stepped out of the shadows of superstition and fear into the moral and spiritual enlightenment of Christian fellowship had become part of him who is the Light of the World (John 8.12).

SONS OF LIGHT

Paul then indulges in another play on words. Christians are SONS OF LIGHT. This Biblical idiom always implies that a man is a son of anything which dominates his character and conditions his nature, e.g. sons of Belial (I Sam. 2.12), sons of this world (Luke 16.8). But since Christians are sons of the Light, which is Christ, they are also SONS OF THE DAY (of Christ), and share in its glory.

BE WAKEFUL AND SOBER

Then, tactfully, Paul changes into the first person before uttering some cautionary words (v. 5b). Although we Christians are children of the light we have no grounds for complacency. We must fit ourselves for our vocation. Let others drowse and dream, we must be alert with our eyes wide open and our wits awake to the moral issues of life. SLEEP, in the sense of a sleeping conscience, and drunkenness, in the sense of irresponsible behaviour, belong to the realm of darkness in which we have no part (v. 7). Nor can we hope to be ready to face the Great Assize unless we have drawn upon supernatural resources. Did not our Lord say: Watch and pray? (Mark 14.38).

THE PANOPLY OF GOD

Therefore let us don the panoply of God (v. 8). The

picture of the Christian warrior goes back to the Old
Testament figure of Yahweh clad for the Judgment in,
among other things, a breastplate of righteousness and a
helmet of salvation (Isa. 59.17). Here the characteristic triad
of Christian virtues appears (cf. 1.3). FAITH and LOVE take
the place of 'righteousness'. HOPE naturally precedes
SALVATION since the whole passage is concerned with this
very thing. Paul uses the metaphor of the Christian arm-
ing himself against the temptations of the world, the flesh
and the devil more fully in Eph. 6.11 ff. Equipped by God's
grace with faith, love, and the hope of salvation the Christian may make his way through the perils of life and be
prepared to face his Judge, in God's good time. For the
whole passage see a close parallel in Romans 13.11-13.

TOGETHER WITH HIM

Although it seems at first as if Paul regards SALVATION
(v. 8) as escape from the DESTRUCTION (v. 3) that overtakes
wrongdoers, or the WRATH (v. 9) of the Judgment, it is
clear from vv. 9-10 that just as he regards WRATH, or
DESTRUCTION, as essentially meaning separation from God,
so he thinks of SALVATION, not as a negative escape from
disaster but as life TOGETHER WITH HIM (i.e. Christ). Once
again the characteristic note is struck of the apostle's fundamental conception of the Christian life as being life ' in
Christ '—in a personal loyalty, commitment and fellowship
which is the only reality in this transitory world order.
Once more his Christian conviction breaks through the
conventional Old Testament symbolism of the Day of
Yahweh.

OUR GROUNDS FOR HOPE

Paul gives us three reasons (vv. 9-10) why as Christians
we can face the dissolution of our bodies or the dissolution

of the present world with equanimity, provided of course
that we have armed ourselves against the evil that surrounds us with the Christian warriors' defences (v. 8) so
that we behave like 'sons of light' and not like 'sons of
darkness'. All of us, good or bad, Christians and non-
Christians, must face eventual Judgment. But Christians
who are in earnest about their faith have more cause to
expect a favourable verdict because (1) God has called us
into his Church; (2) Christ died for us; (3) Christ lives in
us. This is why we have much cause for hope and none
for fear. And this is why, in Paul's view, it is a matter
of indifference to Christian people when the End will
come.

APPOINTED TO SALVATION

(1) It is obvious, so runs his argument, that God cannot
have APPOINTED us (v. 9) to suffer the spiritual annihilation
that faces the enemies of goodness and truth. He has acted
to save us from that fate. He has touched our hearts, and
we have responded. We are within the Christian fellowship,
with all its benefits, not by any virtue of our own but
because God has called us into it. He has given us the
opportunity of obtaining SALVATION, i.e. achieving the perfect relationship to himself, THROUGH OUR LORD JESUS
CHRIST. It is what Christ has done, and what he stiill does,
that makes our salvation possible But this perfect relationship is only a partial relationship here and now. Its full
realization is in the age to come. Hence in the ultimate
sense SALVATION is the opposite of WRATH or DESTRUCTION
and is the substance of Christian hope when the Day of the
Lord comes (Rom. 2.5-11).

CHRIST DIED FOR US

(2) The historical basis of our Christian hope is now

given, namely that Christ DIED FOR US (v. 10). This is the only mention of the Death of Christ for us in the Thessalonian letters and it is not associated with the Resurrection as is normally the case (1.10; 4.14; Rom. 4.25, etc.). It was a fundamental element in the preaching of the early missionaries that Christ died for our sins according to the scriptures (I Cor. 15.3 ff.). The Servant of whom Isaiah had prophesied (Isa. 53) had come and had taken upon himself the sins of the world to bring the world to God. The death of Christ is the focus of his life of self-giving, his ministry of service and love, his entering into human suffering. His obedience was 'unto death'. The perfect response which man should make to God has been made for him by Christ (cf. II Cor. 5.14-21).

AWAKE OR ASLEEP

(3) In the phrase that follows, the Resurrection is implied. It is because Christ rose again from death that we can now LIVE TOGETHER WITH HIM. This life in Christ is our salvation, begun here and consummated hereafter. Whether we WAKE (in life) or SLEEP (in death) we live with him, our Risen and ever-present Saviour. This new relationship with Christ within his Body, the Church—for notice that Paul speaks of life TOGETHER with him: there is no individualistic soul-salvation in Paul's mind—is a relationship which death cannot sever. The Church on earth and in heaven, the Communion of Saints here and hereafter, is for Paul the point of Christ's death (cf. Rom. 14.8-9).

COMFORT ONE ANOTHER

In the case of the Thessalonians to whom these words were originally directed Paul's words here would take them back to their own problems of those who had died

H

before the *Parousia*. He returns to the point which he had
made in 4.14-17. The End will come. When it will come
we cannot tell. But when it does come we need have no
fear that God will have overlooked those who have died
before it. At Christ's coming, the living and the dead, who
have known something of what it means to share his life
in this world, will enter into its full experience in the world
to come. This rounds off the whole eschatological passage
4.13-5.11 and the apostle urges his readers (v. 11) to
take these words to heart and strengthen each other's faith
as indeed they are evidently doing.

THE PROBLEM OF THE TIME FACTOR

If it is not altogether easy for us to enter into the concern of the members of the Thessalonian church about
their dead who might not share in the glory of Christ's
Coming (4.13-18) it is only too easy for us to enter into
their perplexity about the time factor. For them the origin
of this perplexity was the urgency of the missionaries'
appeal based on the impending End of the world; for us it
is the constantly recurring emphasis in the New Testament
on what appears to be an expectancy of an immediate
Parousia—which of course did not take place. Paul's words
here may help us to understand why it was that men caught
up in the Pentecostal atmosphere of the early Church could
speak of the Second Advent as if it were bound to happen
at any moment, but at the same time could proceed to
discourage their converts from being naturally curious to
know at which moment.

'THE LORD IS AT HAND'

The difference lies in the fact that the missionaries shared
the Jewish prophetic certainty of the Triumph of God,
and as their Old Testament predecessors had done, fore-

shortened history by speaking of the end event almost as if it had already happened. If it be true that for God past, present and future are experienceed as an eternal Now, Biblical prophets, who were closer to the mind of God than we are, may well have shared to some degree the divine viewpoint. For Paul, unlike the Thessalonians and ourselves, there seems to have been no difficulty in reconciling the prospect of the *Parousia* in his lifetime with complete unconcern as to the time of its arrival. The truth is that for him the End event was always a present reality. The Lord was always at hand. The time factor hardly entered into his reckoning. What mattered to Paul was that from the moment of their baptism Christians stood under Judgment and in the presence of their Lord. The *Parousia* was to be the full revelation and realization of what this new quality of life meant. When it would happen was relatively unimportant. The Christian's business was to live in such a way as to be able in sober responsibility to share equally a sense of the imminence of Christ's Presence and complete unconcern about its full realization in time.

(c) PROBLEMS OF CHURCH ORDER
5.12-22

Paul now turns from these deeper waters of the Church's eschatological hope to the more practical problems of the day to day conduct of the Church's affairs. The link is his final injunction in v. 11, where he has spoken of the duty of the members of the Church to help each other to a truer understanding of their faith. Now he draws attention to the respect which they owe to their leaders. It may be that the natural independence of the Macedonians was asserting itself in the Christian community and that the rank and file resented any kind of authority.

CHRISTIAN LEADERSHIP

Apparently the practice of the apostle in his missionary journeys was to appoint elders in each new church, after the style of the Jewish synagogues (Acts 14.23), and presumably these are the people referred to here. Paul describes their function generally as pastoral oversight. There is no reason to suppose that because he mentions three aspects of this (v. 12) he has in mind three different officials. Indeed at this early stage the leadership of the church communities cannot be described as a ministry in the modern sense at all, far less an organized hierarchy. It is much rather a picture of naturally gifted members who were best qualified to continue the work of evangelism, to preside over meetings of the community, and to guide its affairs with wise advice.

Their leadership rests on their own merit. They are to be esteemed not because they have been invested with authority but because they are the people who work hardest for the cause of Christ. The phrase enjoining PEACE need suggest no more than the normal storms in the congregational tea-cup. It is clear from the following words (v. 14) addressed to the BRETHREN as a whole, that Paul expected all the members of the community to share pastoral responsibility. What he asks them to do is all too often nowadays regarded as the job of the parson alone.

THE RESPONSIBILITIES OF
CHURCH MEMBERS

The first obligation is rather peculiar to Thessalonica. The word translated by the R.V. as DISORDERLY has been found to have a special meaning which reflects the situation referred to in I 4.11 and II 3.6 ff. A papyrus discovered in Egypt, dating from approximately the same time as this letter, shows that the word means a 'loafer'. It occurs in a contract of apprenticeship in which a father undertakes to see that his son will make up for any time lost through absenteeism. This is therefore an allusion to the need for handling firmly those who have downed tools in preparation for the *Parousia*.

MUTUAL ENCOURAGEMENT

The second pastoral obligation of the members of the congregation towards one another is to ENCOURAGE THE FAINT HEARTED. These are no doubt in this case people who have not found their faith strong enough to withstand the assaults made upon it by persecution (1.6), Jewish malevolence (2.1 ff.), or the death of their loved ones (4.13). But we do not need to go back to Thessalonica to find members in every congregation whose faith has been tested almost to breaking point by the chances and changes of life, and who need all the help that Christian friendship can give.

HELP AND SYMPATHY

Thirdly there are the WEAK who need support. In a sense this includes every member of every church since the beginning of Christianity. The Church exists, as we are constantly reminded, not for saints but for sinners. But there are those who by nature or by grace are stronger characters than others and who by their example and practical service can help others to keep their feet on the slippery places of life. The laxity of twentieth-century standards is a more insidious temptation than the blatant paganism on which the Thessalonian Christians had once turned their backs. But the broad way downwards has always a strong pull for some, so 'put your arm around them', says the apostle, 'be patient with all of them'. The

first requisite in helping others is to try to understand why
they need help, and to share their problem.

WIDER ISSUES

The next injunction (v. 15) goes beyond the life of the
congregation or of the Church at large and is one of the
revolutionary Christian maxims which remind us that
Christianity demands more than justice. Revenge is still as
instinctive a reaction as when it was embedded in the Old
Testament code (Ex. 21.24 ff.). But Jesus has set us a
new standard (Matt. 5.44), however much we come short
of it. Paul echoes it elsewhere (Rom. 12.17), as does the
first epistle of Peter (3.9). While at Thessalonica the temptation must have been to pay back, when opportunity
offered, some of the hurt done by Jews and Gentiles (2.14),
we may well take this in the widest sense as the Christian
duty in the world at large to stand for the exercise of
charity, mercy and peace-making in the whole range of
public questions from capital punishment to international
relations. The aim of the Christian must always be to
secure the greatest GOOD for ALL.

JOY

Then follow (vv. 16-18) what have been called the
' standing orders of the Christian Church '. REJOICE ALWAY,
says the apostle, himself a man who had had all too often
more cause for tears. And he says it to men who, as is clear
from these letters, were pursuing no rose-strewn path. But
this is the Christian paradox which shines out on every
page of the New Testament that neither Jewish opposition
nor Gentile persecution could repress the gaiety of the
early Church. In contrast to the stranglehold of Judaism
or the hopelessness of paganism, converts to Christianity
shared the exhilaration of free men—freedom from fear,

from guilt, from frustration and from despair. No one felt this more strongly than Paul and the call to rejoice is often on his lips. Its roots lie in the deep region of fellowship with Christ and in the certainty of soon being for ever with the Lord (4.13).

PRAYER

To PRAY WITHOUT CEASING (v. 17) does not mean a perpetual badgering of God with our petitions—although our Lord encourages us to take to him our smallest concerns—but rather a permanently open heart and mind to receive the messages that God sends us. The great saints have always tended to think of prayer as listening. This is the attitude of worship which makes work and play an offering to God. It is not necessary to live in a monastic order to have a life that is dominated by prayer. No one proved the efficacy of constant prayer in the hurly-burly of a rootless world more than Paul himself.

THANKSGIVING

The third of the standing orders is to GIVE THANKS for EVERYTHING (v. 18). This is the fruit of a realization that all things—good and bad, joys and sorrows, triumphs and tragedies—work together for good to them that love God (Rom. 8.28). Presumably since Paul has just mentioned prayer he is not thinking of thanksgiving as an element of formal prayer but rather as an attitude of grateful acknowledgment that all that we have—life, health, food, home—comes from God. If we see his hand in the pleasant things of life, should we not also look for his leading in the mischances that befall us?

THE PATTERN AND THE POWER

These three elements of the Christian life—joy, prayer,

thanksgiving—as the apostle presents them here have only once been woven into the perfect pattern of man as God meant man to be. In the revelation of himself and his WILL for us in CHRIST JESUS God has shown us once and for all what human life should be like. In the fellowship of the Body of Christ he gives us a foretaste of how the apparently impossible demands made by the gospel can begin to be met, and a foreshadowing of their perfect realization in the age to come.

THE GIFTS OF THE SPIRIT

The last words that Paul has to say about the conduct of church life here (vv. 19-22) take us into the heart of the tense atmosphere of the early Church. The life of the new man in Christ, as the apostle has outlined it in vv. 16-18, is only possible through the supernatural power of the Holy Spirit. There were other recognized forms of the Spirit's activity in the early Church, more striking in their operation, but in Paul's view less effective in their ultimate results. He distinguishes the former as the 'fruit' of the Spirit (Gal. 5.22 ff.) and the latter as the 'gifts' of the Spirit, and devotes some time to noting the different types of spiritual 'gifts' in I Cor. 12 and 14. None of them is significant unless it is directed by love which is the chief 'fruit' of the Spirit (I. Cor. 13).

TONGUES AND PROPHECIES

Two of the 'gifts' mentioned in the Corinthian letter, and frequently referred to elsewhere in the New Testament, appear to be involved in vv. 19-22: (1) 'speaking with tongues' (*glossolalia*), which was unintelligible babbling of the Old Testament ecstatic type (I Sam. 19.20-24) such as is still associated with intense emotionalism at religious revivals (v. 19); (2) utterances of a prophetic kind, following the pattern of Amos and his successors, delivered as a result of an abnormal psychic experience (v. 20). Both types were equally regarded as the direct effect of the action of the Holy Spirit (Acts 19.6).

QUENCH NOT THE SPIRIT

It would appear that neither manifestation impressed the Thessalonians, and Paul, although he discourages ' speaking with tongues ' (I Cor. 14) and stresses the importance of a rational and intelligible faith, warns the Church here (v. 19) against the danger of discounting the power of the Spirit or of suppressing it altogether in the life of the congregation. If it is the case that the Thessalonian church, or some of its members, tended to deplore the strange behaviour of those who were seized by this unfamiliar and unattractive frenzy, the apostle's words might tend to make us hesitate in the life of the Church to-day before we condemn forms of religious expression with which we may not sympathize. The ' excesses ' of evangelistic campaigns, or the fervour of sectarian groups may not be acceptable to all of us but may still indicate the presence of the Spirit. We must not DESPISE any ' prophet ' however unlikely his guise or unpalatable the form of his message.

PROVE ALL THINGS

Nevertheless we are not urged to suspend our critical faculties, for Paul goes on to point out that it is equally our Christian duty not to accept blindly any kind of religious excesses as the work of the Spirit without careful examination. In I Cor. 12.10 he insists that it is also a gift of the Spirit to be able to distinguish truth from falsehood, bogus evangelism from the genuine gospel. The crazy utterances of religious cranks inside and outside mental homes must be PROVED, like any other religious manifestation, against the substance of the gospel and the wisdom of the Church. In short, says the apostle (vv. 21-22), use your Christian judgment (I Cor. 14.29) and acknowledge whatever is genuine (GOOD), even if it is expressed in a form you detest, but have nothing to do with what is obviously spurious (EVIL).

V

A FINAL MESSAGE
5.23-28

The letter ends with a prayer and a final salutation. The apostle's prayer (vv. 23-24) is that GOD, who alone has made it possible for men to have the inward PEACE which comes from the knowledge that through Christ he has bridged the gulf which separated sinful humanity from their Creator and Father, might now by his grace enable them to become his true sons and daughters as they were meant to be. Only with God's help and by his indwelling Spirit could they grow into the right relationship between Father and children which Christ had now made possible. This is the process of 'sanctification', which the apostle prays may transform them in every part of their being, so that they may be prepared to face the last encounter of the Judgment unafraid. The distinction between SPIRIT, SOUL and BODY is purely for literary effect, and does not represent any psychological differentiation. This final prayer echoes the thought of the earlier prayer in 3.13.

THE FAITHFULNESS OF GOD

The Christian lives his life under the Judgment of God. Paul has already spoken (v. 8) of the need to don the supernatural armour of faith, hope and love to fit ourselves for the inevitable battle which commitment to Christ involves. The promise of v. 24 is no automatic guarantee that because God has called us into his Church, and renews his call to

119

service every day of our lives, our ultimate sanctification is assured. There is no royal road to the Kingdom of God. What the apostle is saying is that if we do our part and avail ourselves of God's help to live in Christian obedience to him, we may rely on him to keep his promise because he is FAITHFUL. He has set us on the path we should follow: he has shown us our destination: he will help us to get there (v. 24).

PRAY FOR US

Then, as if to remind his readers that the pastor needs the prayers of his people as much as the people need the prayers of the pastor, Paul invites their prayers for himself, Silvanus and Timothy (v. 25). It would also no doubt remind them that life was no easier for Christian missionaries in Corinth than for Christian converts in Thessalonica.

GREETINGS TO ALL

The apostle, as elsewhere, rounds off his letter with a greeting, in this case to the Thessalonian community in general, but including everyone, even the difficult people already hinted at (v. 26). The KISS was the ordinary salutation in the pagan world which was taken over into Christian worship as the 'kiss of peace' symbolizing the unity of the Christian family.

A SOLEMN CHARGE

It is not altogether easy to see why Paul's final charge is so emphatic (v. 27). He adjures the recipients BY THE LORD, a solemn direction, to read the letter to ALL THE BRETHREN, as if they were unlikely to do so or as if some of the brethren were unlikely to want to hear its contents.

Possibly there is no more in this than that he wants the
letter to take the place of the personal visit which has
proved impossible, and further wants to be certain that all
who are involved in the problems dealt with in chs. 4 and 5
should know his mind. Reading aloud was the customary
practice (cf. Acts 8.30) and in Thessalonica no doubt many
members could not read. This injunction seems to imply
that the letter should be taken to them in their homes by
the leaders of the Church and read to them there. It was
of course as a result of reading Paul's letters aloud at
meetings of the church communities and passing them
round from church to church that they came to have a
place alongside the gospels in the canon of the New
Testament.

The letter ends as it began with a prayer that the grace
of Christ might be with the church (v. 28).

THE SECOND EPISTLE
TO THE THESSALONIANS

I

GREETING
1.1-2

The greeting (vv. 1-2) of the second letter follows the pattern of that of the first. Silvanus and Timothy are once again associated with Paul in sending a goodwill message to their friends in Thessalonica. A few weeks have passed since the first letter was written. The apostle—still in Corinth—has somehow learned that some of the points made in his previous letter have not been properly understood and he is obliged to write again. But the situation both of the missionaries and the members of the Thessalonian community appears to be largely unchanged. We should therefore expect a certain amount of repetition in the framework and general sentiments.

THANKSGIVING
1.3-4

The thanksgiving (vv. 3-4) which comes after the greeting in the normal style of letters in those days is, if anything, more fervent than in the first letter. Whatever minor correctives may be necessary to enable some members of the Thessalonian church to reach a truer understanding of the Second Advent, there is no question of the general excellence of their record. WE ARE BOUND TO GIVE THANKS does not in any way suggest reluctant praise, but rather that the apostles cannot refrain from expressing once more their

I

gratitude to God for the wonderful witness of FAITH and
LOVE which the little community is making.

THE MIRACLE AT THESSALONICA

Paul had not confined himself to conventional congratulation of the Thessalonian church in his last letter. It may
well be that he had heard in the meantime that they
modestly deprecated his enthusiastic commendation and
that he now feels obliged to assure them that he meant
every word of it and more. Whatever the Thessalonians
thought of themselves Paul's uppermost thought was of
the miracle that God had wrought in transforming men
and women who had been enmeshed in the sensuous and
superstitious web of paganism into a closely knit band of
brothers in Christ, outstanding for their service of one
another and their devotion to the God whom they had
come to know.

He realized only too well from his own experience that
loyalty to Jesus was no easy matter. At Thessalonica the
opposition mentioned in the first letter (I 2.14; I 3.3)
apparently continued unabated (v. 4). But the tough
resistance (PATIENCE) of the little church to Jewish provo-
cation and Gentile violence and their trust in God through
all their troubles were a source of pride to Christians
everywhere.

THE MORAL ORDER OF THE UNIVERSE
1.5-7a

Then Paul goes on (vv. 5-7a) to remind us that since it
is God's world we live in, we should look for signs of his
activity even in the seamy side of experience. There is a
moral order in the universe. That and not the adversities
which afflict us is the reality which we as Christians must

hold on to. In the case of the Thessalonians opposition came from the machinations of the enemies of the gospel, doubtless in some cases moved by genuine conviction, but in most cases by sheer malice and resentment. In the twentieth-century world, whether it be the persecution of Christians by hostile governments, or in more fortunate countries like our own the daily battle against the self-interest, prejudice, greed and ill-will which make the Christian life a heartbreaking struggle for so many, Paul's words are a salutary antidote to despondency and despair.

MAN'S DISORDER

As Christians, we cannot believe the gospel and at the same time believe that this is life as God meant it to be. The freedom which he has given to men to choose good or evil inevitably leads to injustice and suffering. At times it seems as if God has forsaken his people. Yet in their hearts Christians know that is not true and can never be true, and that in the end God's love will triumph over the sinful pride of men and the misery that it brings to human kind. The ultimate rule of God beyond this present age, on which we fix our hope, means perfect union with him for those who follow faithfully the path that Christ has pointed and has himself marked out with the prints of his wounded feet. That is the REST (v. 7a) that awaits us.

THE POINT OF NO RETURN

But since God is just, and governs his universe according-ly, the ultimate end of those who deliberately choose to flout the gospel and the ample warnings of scripture and history is spiritual death and final separation from God. Every action that is contrary to the will of God, consciously embarked on and unrepented, widens the gulf between a man and his Maker. Paul reminds us that God is not

mocked, that there is a point of no return on the road that
is paved with pride, self-will, hatred and the other sins of
the spirit, and that the day to day choices that men make
determine whether the future holds eternal life with God
or eternal death without him. It is clear when we look at
v. 9 that Paul is not thinking in v. 6 of eternal torment but
of eternal extinction.

THE FINAL WORD IS WITH GOD

Meantime let those who suffer for Christ's sake take
heart (v. 5). Their afflictions are strengthening their moral
fibre and enriching their character. They are being made
WORTHY of their final place among the redeemed saints of
God. The very fact that they are being enabled to bear their
trials with fortitude, and that they find themselves upheld
by a power beyond their own, is proof that the evil things
of this age will be conquered in the age to come. Their
inward strength and their victory over all opposition is a
foretaste of that ultimate victory of God over his enemies
at the end of time. They know here and now that despite
the apparent injustices of life the last word is with God.

THE LAST ASSIZE
1.7b-10

While it is true that in this age the wicked sometimes
get their deserts and their innocent victims are vindicated,
Paul is enough of a realist not to underestimate the power
of evil in the world as we know it. Consequently he looks
to the Final Judgment as the time when those who have
suffered unjustly in this world will be vindicated and evildoers will reap the reward of their crimes. In the following
verses (7b-10) he draws a vivid pen-picture of the Last
Assize. It is couched in the traditional imagery of the Old

Testament, but here as elsewhere in these eschatological passages we must regard it as an impressionist portrayal rather than as literal prediction. It is in effect a dramatic presentation of the theological conviction which has just been expressed in vv. 5-7a, namely that our actions here and now, be they good or bad, have eternal significance and eternal consequences.

AN OLD TESTAMENT SETTING

The theme is the Day of the Lord, the Old Testament conception of the vindication of God's supremacy, translated into Christian terms. Christ appears in glory with a heavenly retinue to judge mankind and apportion reward or punishment. It is a graphic picture, embellished with conventional symbolism. Two comments may be made at once. Firstly, that compared with the normal apocalyptic imagery of the inter-testamental period, Paul's picture is notable for its restraint and reticence. Here we have none of the lurid details of the torments of the damned or the smug satisfaction of the saved, in which the Renaissance painters and sculptors delighted. Secondly, Paul's conception is not that of an arbitrary distribution of rewards and punishments in accordance with the Judge's decision.

THE CONSEQUENCES OF SIN

Although he uses words like VENGEANCE, PUNISHMENT, DESTRUCTION, it is clear from v. 9 that for him this means not retaliation on the part of an outraged Deity, but rather that in our final encounter with God the inevitable consequences of our past actions come into effect. When Christ is ultimately revealed in his glory we see ourselves as we are and as we have made ourselves. Whether we have fitted ourselves to live with him for ever, or whether by our sin and failure we cannot bear to face him, the Last Judg-

ment is but the summing up of the judgment we have
brought upon ourselves by our day to day behaviour. The
Judgment is essentially the differentiation of those who
have chosen life in Christ with its eternal consequences
from those who have made themselves unable to share it.

THE MOMENT OF REVELATION

In the light of this we may now turn to vv. 7b-10 with
less danger of losing sight of Paul's main emphasis. The
Second Coming of Christ from HEAVEN is the moment
of REVELATION when all men, not only Christians, see him
as he really is: not as the crucified Carpenter but as God
in power and glory. This inexpressible glory is pictorially
suggested by the presence of the angelic host and FLAMING
FIRE, as when Yahweh descended on Sinai (Deut. 33.2).

WRONG CHOICES

His mission will be to punish (as was said of Yahweh in
Isaiah 66.15) all who flout the guidance of conscience (as
in I 4.5) and all who turn their backs upon the gospel
(v. 8). Although this is said with special reference to the
persecution of the Christians at Thessalonica by Gentiles
and Jews, the application is universal. We do not bring
judgment upon ourselves by being ignorant of God or the
gospel, but by refusing to recognize (KNOW) the elementary
natural laws common to all mankind or by rejecting the
truth in Christ when it is presented to us.

THE PUNISHMENT OF SEPARATION

The result of that, the PUNISHMENT (v. 9) is separation
(DESTRUCTION) for ever FROM THE FACE OF THE LORD AND
FROM THE GLORY OF HIS MIGHT. Paul is quoting here almost
verbatim from the description of the Day of the Lord in

Isaiah 2.10, 19, 21, except that he significantly omits the
element of 'terror'. His thought is that, at the final encounter with the power and majesty of God, those who
have chosen to separate themselves from God in this life
will realize to the full in the life to come what separation
from God really means. They will not only see God as he
really is, but themselves as they really are.

HEAVEN AND HELL

They will know then that they have failed to fulfil their
destiny as sons and daughters of God. That will be their
Hell, a Hell in which they have lived on earth, consciously
or unconsciously, but which will then at last be known for
what it is. On the other hand when in the End (IN THAT
DAY) Christ gathers his followers around him (v. 10) and
the faithful witness of the members of his Church adds
lustre to his Triumph, they for their part will know that
the life in Christ which they began to share on earth is the
Heaven in which they will live for ever.

PAUL'S PRAYER
1.11-12

Paul ends the first part of his letter (vv. 11-12) with a
prayer (cf. I 3.12-13). As he contemplates the picture before
his eyes of the final act in the divine drama, the end of
history and the indescribable glory of the Victorious Christ,
he asks that God may so bring to fruition every good
impulse, and every loving thought which he plants in the
hearts of his people, that at the last they may be WORTHY
of all that he has done for them, and be a credit to the
Lord whom they have begun to serve. Only the GRACE of
Father and Son can make this possible.

ANTICHRIST
2.1-12

The preliminary business having been disposed of, Paul turns now to the first of the two special problems which occasioned this letter. Both are connected with misunderstandings as to the date of the *Parousia*. In the first case it appears that Paul had been somehow misrepresented as saying that the End of the World was actually upon them, with the result that there was general excitement and confusion in the Thessalonian church. Paul deals with this (2.1-12) by reminding his readers of the recognized preludes to the End, none of which was apparent. In the second case, where a number of the church members had downed tools in some kind of Second Advent hysteria, the apostle recommends hunger as the treatment best calculated to bring them to their senses (3.6-15).

AN INSOLUBLE PROBLEM

In contrast to the blunt realism of the second passage, this section (2.1-12), dealing with the indications which may be expected to herald the end of the world, provides us with the weirdest piece of writing in all the epistles and one that has never yet been satisfactorily explained. Nor is it likely that it ever will be. There is so much in this passage which is left unsaid and taken for granted. From v. 5 it is clear that a good deal had been included in the teaching of the missionaries during the initial campaign which is here assumed, and which we have now no means of knowing. Judging by the nature of what little Paul does mention of the fantastic apocalyptic signs of the End it is small wonder that the Thessalonians had failed to grasp it.

AUGUSTINE AND AFTER

Even the master mind of Augustine confessed failure in the attempt to elicit the correct interpretation of the passage. 'We, who do not know what they knew, desire and yet are unable even with all our efforts to get at what the apostle meant, especially as the things which he adds make his meaning still more obscure.' Since his day speculation has been endless and to deal with the variety of solutions that have been propounded would take us far beyond the scope of this commentary. F. W. Farrer speaks of them as 'that vast limbo of exploded exegesis—the vastest and the dreariest that human imagination has conceived'.

THE SITUATION AT THESSALONICA

Paul begins by referring (v. 1) to the picture that he had drawn in his previous letter of the reunion of Christ with his people at his Triumph (I 4.16 f.). What he has to say refers to this event, and his message is that there is no ground for imagining that this moment has arrived (v. 2). Apparently for some reason the Thessalonians had come to believe that the DAY OF THE LORD was actually upon them, and the little community was naturally considerably SHAKEN with excitement and apprehension. However easy it was for Paul, like the Old Testament prophets, to think and speak of the DAY OF THE LORD as an imminent event while at the same time calmly pursuing his normal activities, a similarly confident faith could hardly be expected from less theologically minded and recently converted pagans.

FALSE RUMOURS

It is not clear what had convinced the Thessalonians that
the period of crisis, which would come to a climax with
the appearance of Christ, had already begun. Paul does not
seem to know. But it appears to have been connected with
some statement purporting to come from him. It was something he was alleged to have said in a moment of prophetic
insight (SPIRIT), in a sermon (WORD) or in a letter. At all
events, he goes on, they must not allow themselves to be
led astray by rumours from any source whatever (v. 3).
They ought to remember what he had told them during
the campaign (v. 5) that the End would be heralded by the
Rebellion (FALLING AWAY) and the appearance of the MAN
OF SIN (v. 3). Until these things happened the *Parousia*
would not take place.

THE REBELLION AND THE MAN OF SIN

The FALLING AWAY, or Rebellion, seems to be a reference
to the expectation, common to Jewish and Christian teaching about the end of history, that it would be heralded by
widespread apostasy from God (cf. II Esdras 5.1 ff.; Matt.
24.10 ff.). This was to be one of the unnatural portents
by which men would know that THE DAY OF THE LORD was
in sight. Paul points out that this Great Apostasy has not
yet taken place. Nor has the MAN OF SIN appeared. This
perplexing personage, variously described as the 'Man of
Lawlessness' (R.V. margin), the SON OF PERDITION (v. 3),
the LAWLESS ONE (v. 8), together with what Paul tells us
of his activities (vv. 4, 9, 10), sets us an insoluble problem
of interpretation.

ANTICHRIST

A 'man of sin' in the Old Testament idiom is a man

whose nature is essentially sinful. In this case therefore the MAN OF SIN or LAWLESSNESS is someone who is the incarnation of evil. But he is not to be identified with SATAN, for SATAN is his master (v. 9). He is to be REVEALED, as Christ will soon be revealed (1.7), which suggests that there is a close connection between the Advent of Christ and the Advent of the MAN OF SIN. It is basically the conception of Antichrist, although the word is not used in the New Testament before the time of the Johannine epistles (I John 2.18, 22; 4.3; II John 7).

JEWISH ORIGINS

Antichrist is a Christian development from Jewish apocalyptic thought. He is a supernatural figure who embodies evil as the Messiah embodies goodness. Satan is his father, as God is the Father of Christ. He will share the Messiah's supernatural powers (v. 9) and seek to usurp the place and authority of God (v. 4). His coming will precede the coming of the true Christ, who at his *Parousia* will destroy both him and his followers (v. 8, 10). His spirit is even now at work (v. 7a) but his certain end is PERDITION (v. 3), i.e. eternal separation from God.

ANTIOCHUS EPIPHANES

In words reminiscent of the Book of Daniel (7.25; 8.25; 11.36 ff.) he is described as antagonistic to every kind of worship in every kind of religion, and indeed as taking the place of God in the sanctuary and claiming divine honour (v. 4). The cryptic allusions in the Book of Daniel are based on the historical figure of Antiochus Epiphanes, the Seleucid monarch whose desire to introduce Greek civilization among the 'backward' Jews, whose overlord he was, led to their revolt and the Maccabean war of

independence in 167 B.C. His chief affront to their suscepti-
bilities had been to set up an altar to Zeus in the Temple
at Jerusalem, to cause swine to be sacrificed in the sacred
precincts, and to force the priests to drink the broth. This,
in addition to the public burning of the scriptures and the
prohibition of circumcision and sabbath observance, convinced all orthodox Jews that nothing worse than this
could ever happen and that this must be the prelude to the
end of the world.

PROPHECY AND—

They had come back from exile in Babylon determined
to build up their community in accordance with the laws
of God. And indeed they did so. The *Torah* became the
constitution of the little theocracy in and around the Holy
City. But instead of prospering as the prophets had led
them to believe they would, they remained at the mercy
of whatever great power happened to be in control of
Palestine.

—APOCALYPTIC

As, in consequence of this, their hopes turned to a supernatural intervention of God to usher in the Golden Age
which the prophets had foretold, such an outburst of
sacrilege and violation of the most holy objects of their
faith as the actions of Antiochus involved convinced them
that God would not allow such evil to go unpunished. At
any moment he would show his hand. This wicked world
and its evil men, of whom the worst was Antiochus, himself the incarnation of evil, would be destroyed and the
New Age would begin. It was in this expectation that the
Book of Daniel was written, and when the world did not
come to an end as was expected, this human figure, the
embodiment of evil, became part of the apocalyptic

imagery which was carried over into Christianity and formed the prototype for the idea of Antichrist.

THE DAY OF THE LORD

Elsewhere in the Old Testament, pagan kings, regarded as incarnating the sinful character of their idolatrous peoples, are spoken of as usurping the place of God, and like Antiochus, claiming divine honour (Isa. 14.13-14; Ezek. 28.2). These historical personages, acquiring supernatural attributes in association with the supernatural character of the End of the old age, were woven into the pattern of symbolism associated with THE DAY OF THE LORD. It was inevitable therefore that any similar personage or event on the plane of history after their day should be regarded as a sign of the imminent End. When evil assumed such alarming proportions that God's own authority was challenged the climax could not be far off.

CALIGULA

Such a challenge had been thrown down only ten years before the writing of this letter by the Emperor Caligula, who in A.D. 40 had only been prevented by a calculation of the consequences from carrying out his intention to set up a statue of himself in the Temple at Jerusalem. This logical sequel to the Roman desire to unify their Empire by the political device of Emperor worship, was regarded by the Jews as an act of sacrilege of the same order as that of Antiochus two centuries earlier.

A SUPERNATURAL FIGURE

To Jews and Jewish Christians alike this violation of the sanctuary of God would at once be regarded as an apocalyptic sign. But Caligula cannot be identified with the

MAN OF SIN in this passage, partly because he was by this time already dead and the MAN OF SIN is very much alive; partly because the MAN OF SIN does not merely erect his statue in the Temple, but installs himself there: and partly because the figure of the MAN OF SIN depicted here is clearly of a supra-historical nature.

BEYOND HISTORY

The whole character of apocalyptic writing in general would suggest to us that while historical persons feature in it as a basis for symbolism, the essence of apocalyptic expectation is that it is already moving in a dimension beyond space and time. Antiochus, Caligula, and the Temple at Jerusalem provide the ingredients for a conception which takes us into the realm of a cosmic conflict between the Kingdom of God and the Kingdom of Satan, the final clash between good and evil which to the religious mind, Jewish or Christian, must end in the victory of God.

FALSE TRAILS

Accordingly it is unlikely that any simple historical explanation can be found either of the MAN OF SIN or of the whole passage. For whatever identity we give him—and commentators in the past have not hesitated to equate him with Popes or Puritans according to their particular predilections—no mortal man could be equated with the supernatural elements of this apocalyptic figure. It is hardly necessary to add that any attempt to identify him with political personages, at home or abroad, past, present or future, is equally futile.

THE RESTRAINING POWER

A further problem arises when Paul, having with some

impatience reminded the Thessalonians that they ought to
have remembered what he had told them about the MAN
OF SIN during the mission (v. 5), goes on to reiterate that
this mysterious figure, whose appearance alone would
justify their state of ' End of the World ' excitement, cannot
be revealed in all his horror until some unspecified curb on
his activities (THAT WHICH RESTRAINETH) is removed (v. 6).
His spirit is at work (THE MYSTERY OF LAWLESSNESS) but
so long as the agent of this restraining force (ONE THAT
RESTRAINETH) is still at work, the *Parousia* of the MAN OF
SIN cannot take place (v. 7).

CONFLICTING THEORIES

It is indicative of the impossibility of solving the problem of this whole passage by identifying its various
elements exclusively in terms of contemporary events that
completely contradictory suggestions have been made
towards its interpretation. Up to a point they can all be
substantiated. Thus it has been supposed that the Roman
Empire is personified as the MAN OF SIN, but it has been
equally strongly contended that it is the Roman Empire
that restrains the MAN OF SIN. A similarly cogent case can
be made out for identifying the MAN OF SIN with Judaism,
of for equating the restraining power with the Christian
mission and the ' restrainer ' with Paul himself. By the same
token the arguments against each and all of these interpre-
tations are considerable.

PAULINE APOCALYPTIC

It is difficult to resist the conclusion that the conception
of Antichrist cannot be satisfactorily explained in terms of
contemporary history, although undoubtedly historical
events and personalities enter into it. Like all apocalyptic
writing it is basically a theological conviction expressed in

terms of symbol and image which are irreducible to prosaic historical facts. Paul's theology is throughout an attempt to rethink the faith of the Old Testament in the light of his conversion experience. Apocalyptic expectation was part of that faith and we may be permitted to think that this passage is an example of an early stage in the process of his rethinking along this particular line. Jewish traditions and Christian insights are as yet not wholly assimilated in the mind of the apostle and it would be as difficult to say on the evidence here whether he expected literally the Advent of a supernatural MAN OF SIN, as to say whether he expected a literal fulfilment of the imagery he uses to describe the Second Advent of Christ in v. 8 and elsewhere in these letters.

A THEOLOGICAL CONVICTION

In both cases elements of Old Testament imagery, echoes of words of Jesus, mythological symbolism, and historical allusions may be identified, but the total picture is essentially the expression of a theological conviction, which may perhaps be paraphrased in modern terms in the following way. In the end the Triumph of Christ and his Church is certain. But the road that the Church must travel is a hard one, and the power of evil in the world is a formidable adversary. We have no reason to suppose that the world will get better and better as time goes on, or that Christ's cause will ever lack opposition. Like the Wheat and the Tares in our Lord's parable, good and evil grow and flourish side by side. As man's knowledge and power increase, his capacity to turn them to evil ends develops side by side with his capacity to use them for the good of society.

MAN AND SIN

The symbolism of the final clash between Christ and the

MAN OF SIN represents the ultimate achievement of God's purpose but also the perennial Judgment under which all human activity stands. In daily choice and decision each one of us takes sides either with the DECEIT and lies that lead to perdition or with the TRUTH that leads to SALVATION. It is not too much to read into Paul's imagery the perpetual battle between man as he is and man as he may become through Christ. The MAN OF SIN is the corruption of human nature as it exists in all of us, assuming darker colours in the arch-criminals of history but present in us all as self-will, pride and vanity. The legacy of the mass of human sin which we inherit and the common guilt and failure of society, in which we all share, saddle us with a burden too great for human shoulders.

CHRIST AND SIN

This demonic power of accumulated evil, incarnated in each one of us, can only be defeated by the incarnated goodness of God himself. Only the Second Advent can restore the image of God in distorted human nature. In true Biblical idiom this operation of the Holy Spirit through the Church which will continue throughout history recreating mankind despite the active opposition of the MYSTERY OF LAWLESSNESS is seen by Paul in terms of an ultimate cosmic clash between Christ and Antichrist. The perennial conflict is presented *sub specie aeternitatis* as ending in the undoubted victory of Christ and the final realization of the sovereignty of God. Equally in true prophetic idiom this ultimate battle is presented as close at hand but the practical point which Paul is making in these verses 1-12 is that since there is as yet no sign of Rebellion or Antichrist there is no reason for the Thessalonians to think that the end of the world is upon them.

K

THE PURPOSE OF GOD
2.13-17

In the closing words of the Antichrist passage (vv. 1-12) Paul had been contemplating the sombre fate of those who preferred lies to truth, who rejected the offer of salvation through Christ and, by turning their backs upon the gospel, reached the point where they were unable to distinguish between good and evil (v. 11) and condemned themselves to the sorry end of eternal separation from God. From this gloomy picture he turns thankfully (v. 13) to reassure the Thessalonian Christians that no such thoughts should trouble their minds. Whatever hardships they may now suffer, or whatever anxiety the prospect of the end of the world may cause them, they are God's people and as such have nothing to fear.

THE DIVINE PLAN

As so often happens in Paul's letters some rather trivial occurrence—in this case the Second Advent panic of some of the Thessalonians—is raised on to a high theological plane and becomes the occasion of some of the apostle's most profound insights. He seems to lift these worried and perplexed converts out of the problems of the local situation and to show them what their Christian calling means in the divine plan for mankind. It is no casual chance that makes a man choose Christ rather than Antichrist. We love because he first loved us (I John 4.19) or, as Paul says here, we are responding to an eternal purpose of God that men should find fulfilment of their lives in him. But there is no suggestion here either of predestination or of any mechanical doctrine of election.

FROM THE BEGINNING

A man is a Christian, one of the BRETHREN BELOVED OF THE LORD (Deut. 33.12) because God's intention FROM THE BEGINNING has been that men should have SALVATION, i.e. be brought into the right relationship with himself. There is a variant reading (R.V. margin) attested by good MSS evidence which would give the meaning that God had intended the Thessalonians to be the 'first fruits' of his Son's Church. The translation given in the R.V. text is however more profound and more in keeping with Paul's thought elsewhere (e.g. Rom. 8.28-30; Eph. 1.4). His point is that it was God's purpose in creating the world and man that the universe and all that it contains should be in harmony with him and that man, the crown of creation, should live in fellowship with his Maker and with his neighbour.

GOD'S CALL

In the fact that some men live in that proper relationship, or at least have begun to experience it, while others reject it, Paul does not see any arbitrary choice of God, whereby some are destined for salvation and others for damnation. The apostle has often been misrepresented on this matter. Paul's primary concern in using such a phrase as GOD CHOSE YOU is wholly in line with Old Testament prophecy. It was no merit of Israel that it became the People of God. It was God's loving purpose to save the world through Israel. Similarly no Christian had any right to say anything other than what the publican said in the Temple : God be merciful to me a sinner (Luke 18.13). He had been given the opportunity to enter the Christian fellowship and co-operate with God in his eternal plan to renew the life of the world. In face of this solemn vocation there was no room for self-congratulation, and no ground for regarding a man's conversion to Christianity as anything less than the fulfilment of the divine plan 'before the foundation of the world' (Eph. 1.4).

MAN'S RESPONSE

Paul's next words (v. 14) make it even plainer that he sees nothing automatic or mechanical in the Christian life. A man becomes a Christian as part of the eternal purpose for all mankind. But it is a two-sided process. God summons us but we must respond. In order that his Spirit may work in us, changing us from self-centred twisted mortals into his sons and daughters, we must commit our lives to him in faith. This is what the apostle means by BELIEF OF THE TRUTH. It is the opposite reaction to that of the followers of Antichrist in v. 12.

THE ENCOUNTER WITH CHRIST

It is clear from v. 14 that by TRUTH Paul means no abstract philosophical system. For him the truth is the truth of the GOSPEL of him who said: I am the Way, and the Truth and the Life (John 14.6). It means personal allegiance to Christ. The preaching of the gospel summons us in the realm of time and space to respond to the purpose of God for man's salvation which began before history and ends beyond history. The right relationship to God, begun in response to the proclamation of the GOSPEL and our encounter with Christ, fostered and furthered by the action of his SPIRIT upon us within the fellowship of the Church (BRETHREN) has its end and fulfilment in the society of God's people in the indescribable GLORY of the Age to Come. To become men in Christ here, and to remain loyal to him by God's grace is the path which ends in the fulfilment of our being in the presence of God where we share the depth and wonder of Christ's life and experience.

STAND FAST

Then, as always when Paul has soared to the heights of the mystery of our Christian vocation, he comes back to the practical implications and to the hard facts of daily responsibility (v. 15). He calls on the little community to STAND FAST—not to be upset by rumours of coming disaster or daunted by opposition. They will weather all the stormy and troubled seas that surround them if they will only hold on to the anchor that God has provided— the rules of faith and practice (TRADITIONS) which the apostles had taught them during the mission or had later communicated in writing. This is presumably a reference to I Thess., as opposed to any other letter purporting to come from Paul (cf. v. 2).

WITH GOD'S HELP

But to live the Christian life and trust in God come what may, as Paul has just demanded of his readers, needs more than human strength. So he rounds off this section of his letter with a prayer (vv. 16-17) that Christ, who is mentioned before the Father probably because the apostle's previous thought was of the glory of the Son, and God, who in his love for man sent his Son into the world that we might never lack strength here and hope for the hereafter, might supply the confidence and courage which his people need if they are to do his will.

PAUL ON PARASITES
3.1-18

The third chapter of the second letter to Thessalonica is concerned mainly with the second problem connected with the date of the *Parousia*. This occupies vv. 6-15. The remaining verses introduce the topic (vv. 1-5) and round off the whole letter (vv. 16-18). It is possible that the somewhat disjointed nature of vv. 1-5 may be accounted for if we think of the apostle dictating his reply to a letter which he had received from Thessalonica and touching lightly on some of its contents as his eye lighted on them. But this we cannot tell, and in any case the nature of such items is unknown to us. It is also possible that vv. 1-5 are merely a characteristic Pauline introduction to an awkward topic (I 4.1, 10; 5.11) in which he shares his own problems with his readers and affirms his confidence in the Thessalonian church in general, before going on to deal with the unsatisfactory behaviour of a few of the members.

ENEMIES OF THE FAITH

He begins by asking their prayers for his missionary work in Corinth (vv. 1-2), that the preaching of the gospel may be as successful there as it had been at Thessalonica. When he speaks of the Word 'running' he may be using one of his many metaphors from the Greek games, but more likely it is an echo of Ps. 147.15. He implies that if it is left to spread unhindered the gospel is bound to triumph (BE GLORIFIED) since it has the power of

God behind it. But this does not happen, as they well know. UNREASONABLE AND EVIL MEN try to stop it and prevent its success. Presumably this refers to the vested interests of fanatical Jews and mercenary pagan priests concerned for their livelihood, especially the former (cf. Acts 18.6, 12-17). As the Thessalonians knew only too well, all men are not sympathetic to the Faith (Acts 17.5; I 2.14 ff.). This has also been the costly experience of the whole Church throughout its history.

IN THE POWER OF GOD

But behind the Faith stands God, who guarantees its ultimate victory and who watches over his people and strengthens them against all the assaults of the Devil (v. 3). Whether this refers to the persecution at Thessalonica (1.4) or to some other unspecified temptation is not clear. At all events Paul is confident that as they have hitherto been loyal to the instruction in the Christian life which they have received (2.15) they will also heed the words which he is now going to address to them (vv. 6-15). May God guide them into an ever deeper relationship of LOVE to himself and into a more Christ-like PATIENCE in face of all their difficulties (v. 5).

ABSENTEEISM

The apostle turns now to the problem which is giving him most concern after that of the general excitement caused by an erroneous belief that the Day of the Lord had come (cf. 2.1 ff.). This is a special form of the same hysteria. Paul had already referred to this problem of absenteeism in his earlier letter (5.14) but the trouble seems to have become more acute. Believing that the Lord's Advent was upon them, and that the end was at hand of everything that made up the old world which they knew, some of the church members had apparently downed tools, and were not only living off their fellow Christians but were preventing those who wanted to get on with their own work from doing so.

PAUL'S REMEDY

Having already reassured the Thessalonians on the general question of the date of the *Parousia* by reminding them of what must happen before it takes place (2.1-12) Paul now goes on to prescribe a course of treatment for any who persist in this belief and in consequence behave in a way that brings discredit on the Church as a whole. In the most solemn manner (v. 6) he commands the rest of the community to have nothing to do with these idlers (see note on DISORDERLY in I 5.14). Previously they had been told to warn them, now they are told to ostracize them, to 'send them to Coventry'. They have failed to live up to the standards (TRADITION) required of Christian church membership (I 4.11-12) which the apostles had passed on to them. But because each of them is still a BROTHER there is no suggestion that he should be expelled from the Church.

AN APOSTOLIC EXAMPLE

Paul, as on a previous occasion (I 1.6), urges his readers to take their cue from the behaviour of the missionaries themselves during the campaign (v. 7), and reminds them more or less in the same words as in his previous letter (I 2.9) of how Silvanus, Timothy and he had set them an example of doing an honest day's work to support themselves and be a burden to no one (v. 8). It was not as if they had not been entitled to expect to be maintained by the Church. Our Lord had laid down the principle of voluntary sustentation for his disciples (Matt. 10.9-10) and it was the common practice among itinerant philosophers and preachers. Paul was not above accepting help from his converts when occasion demanded (Phil. 4.16). But the apostles had been determined to set a good example to the Thessalonians (v. 9.).

WORK OR STARVE

Even during the mission campaign the maxim had been laid down that if a man would not work he must go hungry (v. 10). This piece of workshop morality is not distinctively Christian. It might be Jewish or Greek, but in view of the Greek belief that manual labour was only fit for slaves it is more likely to be Jewish. Although Gen. 3.19 regards hard work as part of man's punishment for Adam's disobedience, the rabbis had a high conception of the dignity and importance of physical toil. Here however it is a blunt assertion that a man who is not willing to contribute his quota of effort to the common pool should be allowed to starve.

BUSYBODIES

The specific cause which has given rise to the apostle's stern words is now mentioned (v. 11). Some of the members are reported to have stopped work and to be interfering with the work of other people. A 'busybody' in this case is less likely to mean someone who pries into his neighbour's affairs than someone who has fallen a victim to Second Adventist excitement, has stopped work himself, and now runs around trying to persuade others to do the same. Paul charges all these loafers to get back to work, to calm down and behave sensibly, and to stop sponging off their neighbours (v. 12).

REFORM NOT PUNISHMENT

Behind his next words (v. 13) we can detect a note of sympathy. He urges the rest of the community not to become so exasperated with these irritating people that they forget their Christian duty towards them. They are still their brothers, and obviously they need help. But if gentle admonition and tactful persuasion are unsuccessful, backed up by the powerful authority of this letter, stronger measures must be adopted. The offending members are to be banned from the community until they come to their senses. Paul is confident that shame will bring them back in a more wholesome frame of mind (v. 14). But the purpose of this discipline is reformative, not punitive, because these misguided people are not enemies but brothers (v. 15).

FAIR SHARES

It is possible that the Thessalonians had a natural tendency to be work-shy, especially if some of the membership had been recruited from ' certain vile fellows of the rabble ' (Acts 17.5), and that this was accentuated by misconceptions about the imminent end of the world. But Paul's words here are applicable to a wider audience than the small group at Thessalonica. We could not of course apply his principle of Work or Want without a variety of qualifications to twentieth-century industrial society. He assumes that there is plenty of work available, that the people concerned are all physically fit, and that manual labour alone is involved. But if we make the necessary reservations, his principle that to be self-supporting is a Christian virtue and to be a drone or a parasite is to be less than Christian is still valid. To take more out of the common pool than we put in by our own efforts, whatever our job may be, is to come short of what God demands of us.

CHURCH DISCIPLINE

Still valid likewise is his emphasis on the responsibility of each Christian community for all its members. It is not a matter of indifference to the Church as a whole if some of its members bring the Faith into disrepute. But once more we must recognize that the history of church discipline is a painful one and that as often as not the flagrant and less insidious sins are 'noted' and the members concerned ostracized, or even excommunicated, while the sins of the spirit which do the Church far more harm in the eyes of the outside world pass unchallenged. Divorcees, drinkers, gamblers and sabbath-breakers within the Church are sitting targets. It is doubtful if they have ever done a tenth of the damage that has been done to the cause of Christ by our denominational, political, social and racial intolerance and prejudices.

CLOSING WORDS

Paul concludes the letter, as he began it, with a prayer (v. 16) that Christ, the LORD OF PEACE, might bestow his peace upon the little community, persecuted from without and confused and troubled from within. The significant use of the word ALL includes all whose problems he has tried to meet in the letter.

Then, since it appears that his views had been misrepresented (cf. 2.2), he draws attention (v. 17) to the fact that this is his authoritative ruling on the matter of the Second Advent and the treatment of the BUSYBODIES. Paul's habit was to dictate his letters and sign them with his own hand (I Cor. 16.21; Col. 4.18), which was a distinctive one (Gal. 6.11).

The letter ends with a blessing (v. 18).